# CIRENCESTER
## A HISTORY AND CELEBRATION OF THE TOWN

JUNE R LEWIS-JONES

Produced by The Francis Frith Collection

www.francisfrith.com

First published in the United Kingdom in 2004 by
The Francis Frith Collection®

Hardback Edition 2004 ISBN 1-90493-817-5
Paperback Edition 2011 ISBN 978-1-84589-622-5

Text and Design copyright © The Francis Frith Collection®
Photographs copyright © The Francis Frith Collection®

The Frith photographs and the Frith logo are reproduced under licence from Heritage Photographic Resources Ltd, the owners of the Frith archive and trademarks

All rights reserved. No photograph in this publication may be sold to a third party other than in the original form of this publication, or framed for sale to a third party. No parts of this publication may be reproduced, stored in a retrieval system, or transmitted, in any form, or by any means, electronic, mechanical, photocopying, recording or otherwise, without the prior permission of the publishers and copyright holder.

British Library Cataloguing in Publication Data

Cirencester - A History and Celebration of the Town
June R Lewis-Jones

The Francis Frith Collection®
Oakley Business Park, Wylye Road,
Dinton, Wiltshire SP3 5EU
Tel: +44 (0) 1722 716 376
Email: info@francisfrith.co.uk
www.francisfrith.com

Printed and bound in Great Britain
Contains material sourced from responsibly managed forests

Front Cover: **CIRENCESTER, MARKET PLACE 1898** 40965t

*The colour-tinting in this book is for illustrative purposes only, and is not intended to be historically accurate*

Additional photographs by June R Lewis-Jones
Domesday extract used in timeline by kind permission of Alecto Historical Editions, www.domesdaybook.org.

Aerial photographs reproduced under licence from Simmons Aerofilms Limited.
Historical Ordnance Survey maps reproduced under licence from Homecheck.co.uk

AS WITH ANY HISTORICAL DATABASE, THE FRANCIS FRITH ARCHIVE IS CONSTANTLY BEING CORRECTED AND IMPROVED, AND THE PUBLISHERS WOULD WELCOME INFORMATION ON OMISSIONS OR INACCURACIES

## Contents

| | |
|---|---|
| 6 | Timeline |
| 8 | Chapter 1 : Roman Corinium to Norman Cyrescestre |
| 26 | Chapter 2 : Medieval Monopolies to Georgian Grace and Favours |
| 50 | Chapter 3 : The Victorian Years of Industry and Expansion |
| 74 | Chapter 4 : 1900-2000 A Century of Change |
| 102 | Chapter 5 : The Town Today: Modern Life Built on Ancient Foundations |
| 116 | Acknowledgements |
| 117 | Bibliography |
| 121 | Free Mounted Print Offer |

CIRENCESTER FROM THE AIR 1939 AFR6311

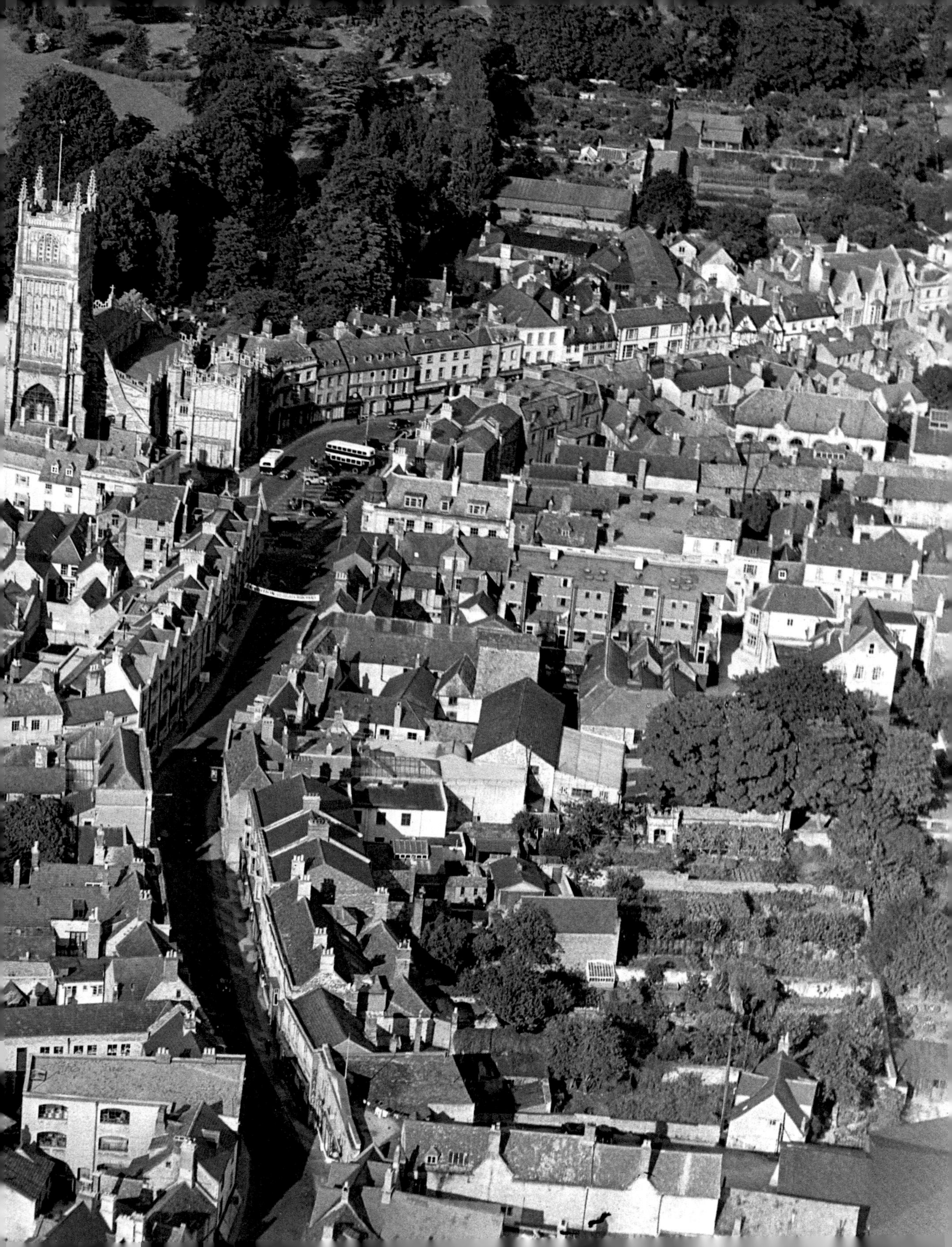

CIRENCESTER – *a history and celebration of the town*

# Historical Timeline for Cirencester

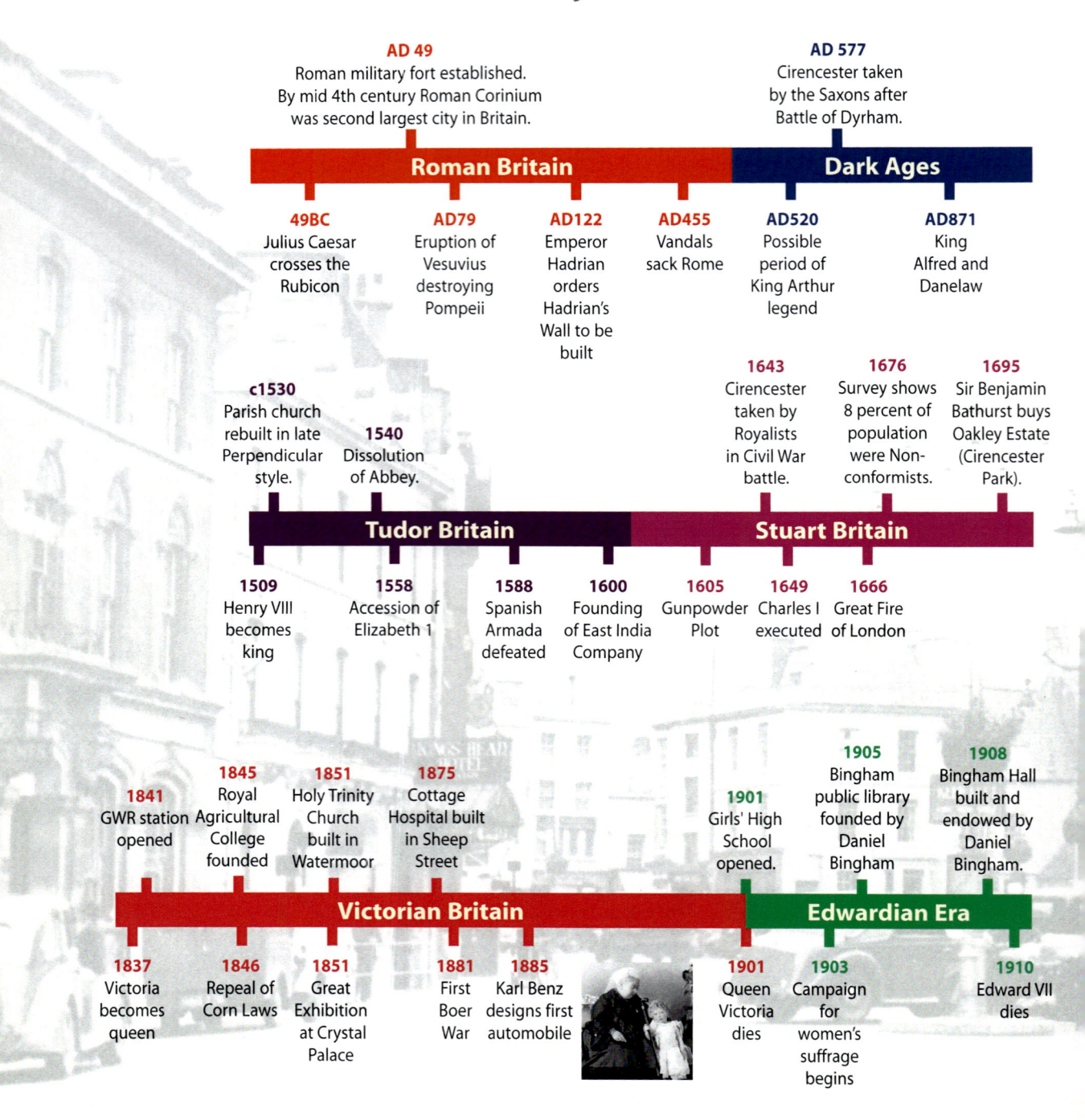

## Roman Britain / Dark Ages

- **AD 49** — Roman military fort established. By mid 4th century Roman Corinium was second largest city in Britain.
- **AD 577** — Cirencester taken by the Saxons after Battle of Dyrham.

- **49BC** — Julius Caesar crosses the Rubicon
- **AD79** — Eruption of Vesuvius destroying Pompeii
- **AD122** — Emperor Hadrian orders Hadrian's Wall to be built
- **AD455** — Vandals sack Rome
- **AD520** — Possible period of King Arthur legend
- **AD871** — King Alfred and Danelaw

## Tudor Britain / Stuart Britain

- **c1530** — Parish church rebuilt in late Perpendicular style.
- **1540** — Dissolution of Abbey.
- **1643** — Cirencester taken by Royalists in Civil War battle.
- **1676** — Survey shows 8 percent of population were Non-conformists.
- **1695** — Sir Benjamin Bathurst buys Oakley Estate (Cirencester Park).

- **1509** — Henry VIII becomes king
- **1558** — Accession of Elizabeth 1
- **1588** — Spanish Armada defeated
- **1600** — Founding of East India Company
- **1605** — Gunpowder Plot
- **1649** — Charles I executed
- **1666** — Great Fire of London

## Victorian Britain / Edwardian Era

- **1841** — GWR station opened
- **1845** — Royal Agricultural College founded
- **1851** — Holy Trinity Church built in Watermoor
- **1875** — Cottage Hospital built in Sheep Street
- **1901** — Girls' High School opened.
- **1905** — Bingham public library founded by Daniel Bingham
- **1908** — Bingham Hall built and endowed by Daniel Bingham.

- **1837** — Victoria becomes queen
- **1846** — Repeal of Corn Laws
- **1851** — Great Exhibition at Crystal Palace
- **1881** — First Boer War
- **1885** — Karl Benz designs first automobile
- **1901** — Queen Victoria dies
- **1903** — Campaign for women's suffrage begins
- **1910** — Edward VII dies

## Middle Ages

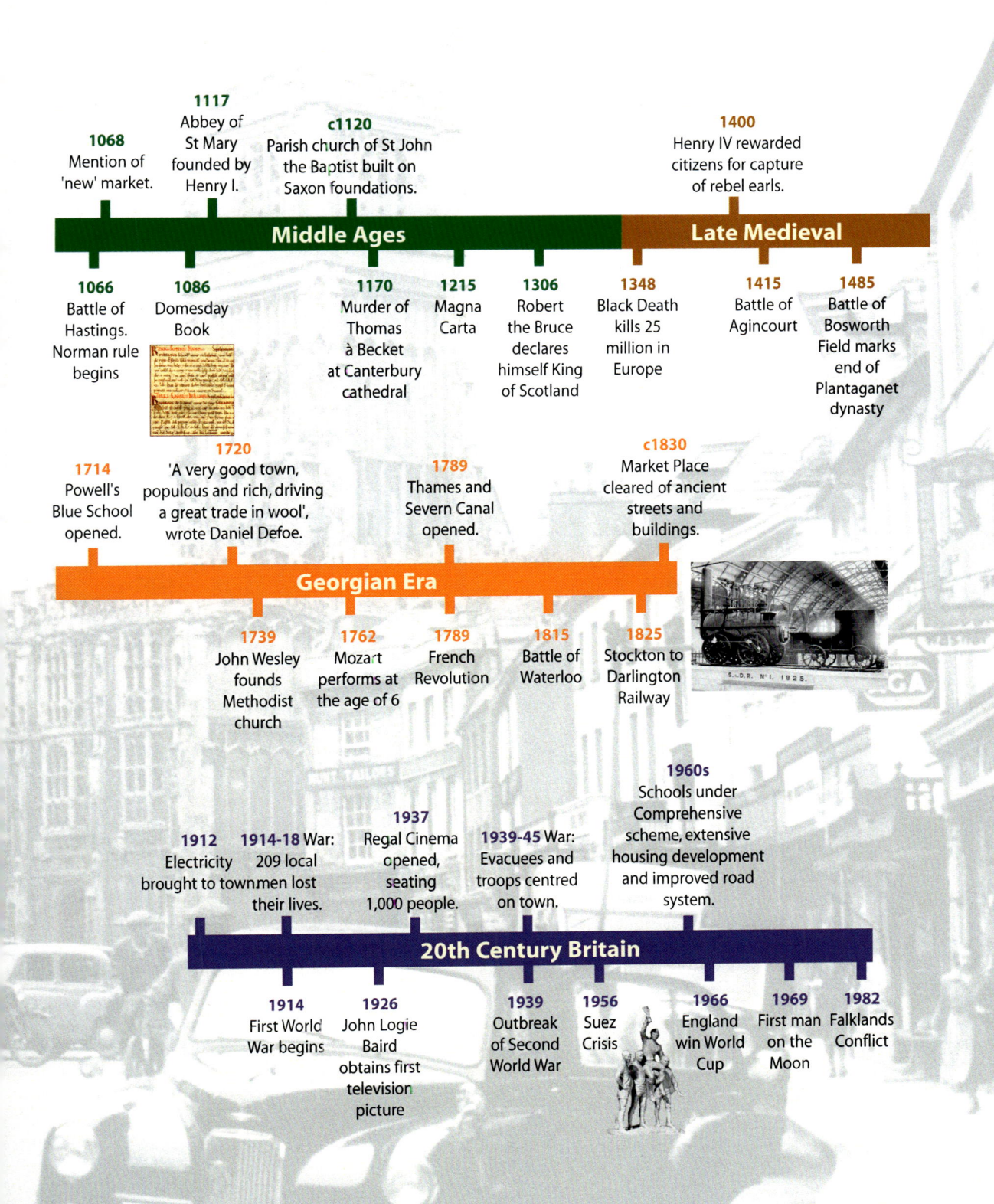

**1068** Mention of 'new' market.

**1117** Abbey of St Mary founded by Henry I.

**c1120** Parish church of St John the Baptist built on Saxon foundations.

**1066** Battle of Hastings. Norman rule begins

**1086** Domesday Book

**1170** Murder of Thomas à Becket at Canterbury cathedral

**1215** Magna Carta

**1306** Robert the Bruce declares himself King of Scotland

## Late Medieval

**1400** Henry IV rewarded citizens for capture of rebel earls.

**1348** Black Death kills 25 million in Europe

**1415** Battle of Agincourt

**1485** Battle of Bosworth Field marks end of Plantaganet dynasty

## Georgian Era

**1714** Powell's Blue School opened.

**1720** 'A very good town, populous and rich, driving a great trade in wool', wrote Daniel Defoe.

**1789** Thames and Severn Canal opened.

**c1830** Market Place cleared of ancient streets and buildings.

**1739** John Wesley founds Methodist church

**1762** Mozart performs at the age of 6

**1789** French Revolution

**1815** Battle of Waterloo

**1825** Stockton to Darlington Railway

## 20th Century Britain

**1912** Electricity brought to town

**1914-18** War: 209 local men lost their lives.

**1937** Regal Cinema opened, seating 1,000 people.

**1939-45** War: Evacuees and troops centred on town.

**1960s** Schools under Comprehensive scheme, extensive housing development and improved road system.

**1914** First World War begins

**1926** John Logie Baird obtains first television picture

**1939** Outbreak of Second World War

**1956** Suez Crisis

**1966** England win World Cup

**1969** First man on the Moon

**1982** Falklands Conflict

ANTIQUES
F. J. COLE
GUNMAKERS
SPORTS OUTFITTERS
TOYS
A.J.GORRINGE

CHAPTER ONE

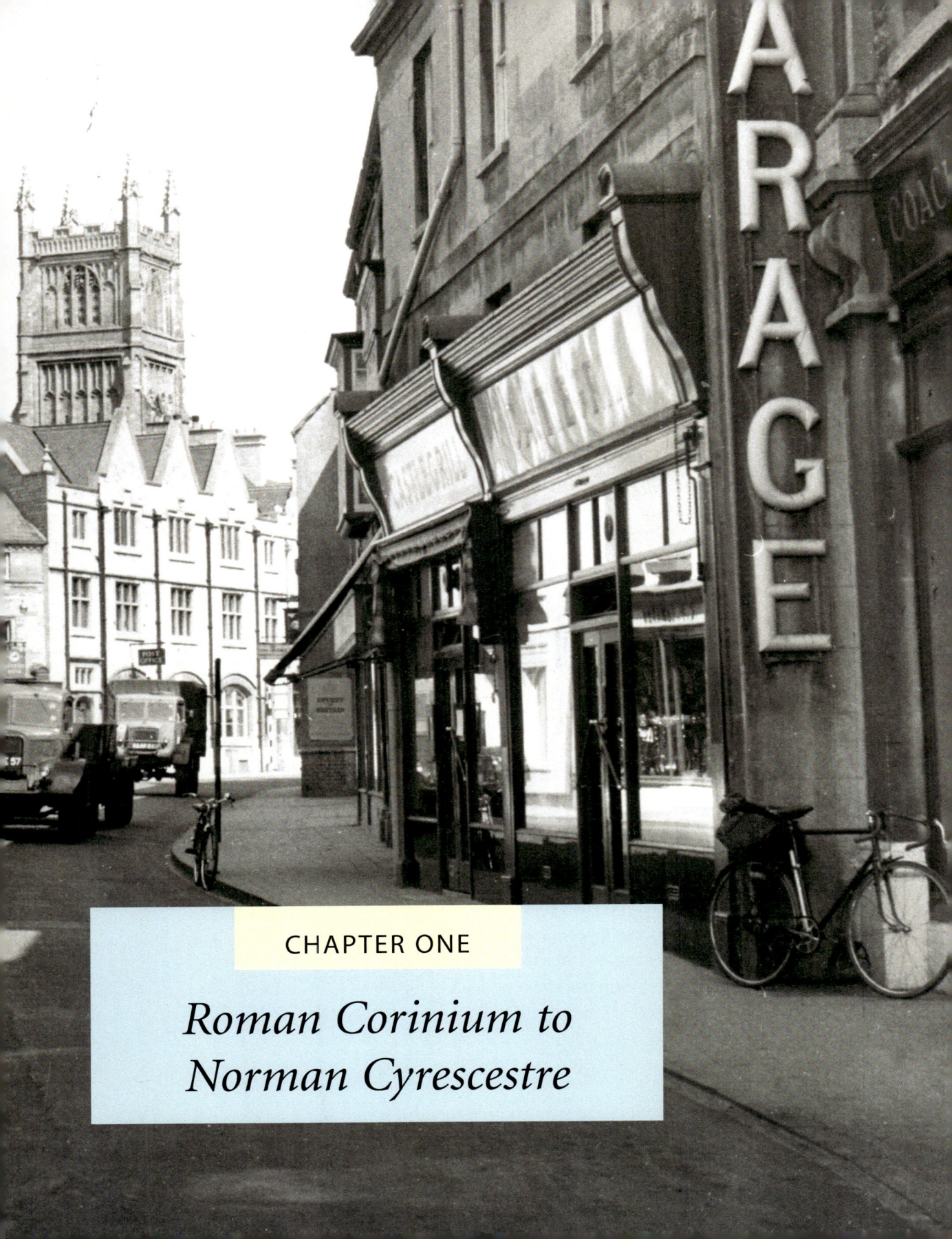

*Roman Corinium to Norman Cyrescestre*

'SCRATCH GLOUCESTERSHIRE and find Rome' is a well-worn local saying, and archaeological excavations, often prompted from chance finds of tesserae unearthed from mosaic floors, a tessellated corridor or hypocaust foundations, have produced valuable and tangible evidence of how this south-eastern corner of the Cotswolds was created to become part of a new Roman province following the invasion of AD 43, with Cirencester as the capital of Britannia Prima. Only London was larger in the whole of Roman Britain.

The Romans called their city Corinium. Ptolemy, the Greek geographer, writes of it around AD 150 as Korinion; 500 years later it was recorded as Cironium; in succeeding documents it appears as Cirrenceastre and Cyrneceastre, and in the Domesday reckoning as Cyrescestre. Some 50 variants of spelling have been noted over a millennium, up until the present-day Cirencester, with many of the older generation, 'county folk', clerics and lawyers favouring Shakespeare's Ciceter (which rhymes with 'solicitor' and 'visitor'). Locals abbreviate it affectionately to Ciren, with a soft sibilant 's'. The association between the name of the town and that of the River Churn around which it developed is not therefore immediately apparent, but is revealed when we discover that in ancient times the letter 'c' was pronounced 'ch'. The Normans, showing true French aversion to the 'ch' sound, preferred to say 'ts' - which eventually became 's'. The exception is for the River Churn, and that is pronounced as it is spelt.

**MARKET PLACE 1898** 40964

*Roman Corinium to Norman Cyrescestre* 11

Cirencester was the second largest city in Roman Britain.

## The Town's Museums

The building on the left-hand-side corner was the Museum of Roman Antiquities, built by the 4th Earl Bathurst in 1856 to house his private collection, which was later donated to the town when the new museum was built. The Old Museum has since served many purposes: until recently the Town Band held their practice sessions there, and it has now been converted for use as offices. The Corinium Museum was purpose built at the back of premises formerly used by the YMCA, and presented to the Urban District Council for the town by the Earl and Countess Bathurst and Sir Frederick Cripps. It was opened by Professor George M Trevelyan in November 1938.

**APPROACH FROM TETBURY ROAD c1960** C106122

*Roman Corinium to Norman Cyrescestre*

**ENTRANCE TO THE CORINIUM MUSEUM 2004**
C106701k (June Lewis-Jones)

The entrance archway, with Ionic columns and entablature, was based on the design of a Roman temple, making a fitting introduction to what has become an award-winning museum where groups and individuals can take an active part in finding the all-important links between the past and present.

Much of Roman Corinium lies beneath modern-day Cirencester. Thanks to the enthusiastic and dedicated archaeologists who have painstakingly and literally dug into the past, an amazing and extensive picture of the town and the life of its inhabitants has been revealed so that we can study, enjoy and understand more fully our long and valued heritage. Although Cirencester has a rich legacy of Roman remains, the town is not a living museum. Artefacts, mosaics and an absorbing interpretation of the life and times of the town over 2,000 years make an unrivalled collection in the appropriately named Corinium Museum in Park Street.

Continued use of the name Corinium helps to perpetuate Cirencester's Roman roots. It is used to identify several local organisations (from ladies' luncheon clubs to karate clubs) and is a popular trade name (from firms supplying replacement windows to a school of driving). In addition, numerous buildings (both private residences and estate developments) proudly incorporate Corinium in their address. To literally follow in the footsteps of those ancient town dwellers at ground level there is no better place to start than at appropriately named Corinium Gate. Situated on the northeast side of the town, Corinium Gate was one of at least four gates within the encircling walls of the Roman city, and its site is marked by a plaque on the Cotswold-stone wall on the London Road, opposite the Beeches car park. The plaque reads:

'On this site stood the north-east gate of Roman Corinium where the Fosse Way from

**THE RIVER CHURN AND THE LONDON ROAD 2004** C106702k *(June Lewis-Jones)*

The Churn goes under the London Road alongside the Beeches car park, from where this view was taken. The London Road leads out of the town to the ancient Roman Fosse Way.

Lincoln and Akeman Street from Verulamium (St Albans) entered the town. Excavation in 1960 revealed a gate 30m wide with flanking towers and a dual carriageway of cobbled streets. The River Churn was diverted to flow just outside the town wall.'

If you enter by way of Corinium Gate (now a leafy residential area) into the historic abbey grounds, then cross two small bridges, you come to the exposed remains of Roman walls. These are thought to have been built in the second century AD, for in the early years under Roman rule the town had no defences. It was during this later period that Corinium developed into a principal military fort, strategically placed on the major route of the Fosse Way, at the convergence of Akeman Street and Ermin Street, and utilising the ancient salt route of the Whiteway. The ancient Britons in the area, the Dobunni, whose centre was at Bagendon, some four miles north of Cirencester, had surrendered to the invaders, and they and their tribal name were integrated eventually into the new and powerful city of Corinium Dobunnorum. Fortified Cirencester, on its low plateau and settled within the hills to the south and west, was easily defended.

# Roman Corinium to Norman Cyrescestre

**ARTIST'S IMPRESSION OF A ROMAN HELMET, FOUND IN GERMANY** F6014

After some two decades of military occupation the Roman cavalry left to join the force pushing westward. A collection of Samian ware is among a varied range of everyday objects found in the area showing something of how the Romans lived - and preserved in the Corinium Museum are two tombstones erected to soldiers who never returned to their homeland. One shows, in sculptured relief, a cavalryman mounted on a sturdy high-stepping horse; from the inscription we learn that Dannicus was of the Indiana regiment. His image affords us some visual form of identity of at least one of those early people.

Following the dismantling of the military garrison a new civil and commercial centre was built, with the Basilica as the principal public building. It was from here the affairs of the local community were administered by an elected council, drawn mainly from the native Dobunni under Roman supervision. It was located in the area off The Avenue, bounded by the Masonic Hall and the entrance to St Michael's Field. On the northwest side of the Basilica was the Forum, a large paved courtyard where townsfolk gathered to hear the latest news and proclamations on matters of law or simply chat to friends. A covered colonnade edged the Forum on three sides, leading to shops and business premises and, perhaps, public baths - although to date none has been discovered here.

The Corinium Museum is a treasure house of artefacts that bring Cirencester under Roman rule to life. In particular, fine mosaic floors, stone sculptures and a reconstructed kitchen give an insight into the culture, craftsmanship and civilisation of the time. Wealthy Romans enjoyed fresh local produce such as vegetables, wheat and meat, enhanced for their more sophisticated taste by good wine, herbs and spices, and oil imported

## The Hare Mosaic

**CORINIUM MUSEUM 2004** C106703k (June Lewis-Jones)

The Hare, nibbling at a bunch of grapes, is a typical Mediterranean design, but is the only one of its kind found in England. It has become both the logo for the Corinium Museum and an important town symbol, and is replicated as the central motif in the Brewery courtyard.

# The Hare Mosaic

**DAVID VINER AND THE HARE MOSAIC** ZZZ00394 *(June Lewis-Jones)*

David Viner was Curator of the Corinium Museum for 27 years, working amongst its fine collections of antiquities. What impressed him most were the exquisite mosaics, especially 'The Hare'. The photograph above shows him with this mosaic, shortly after it had been mounted for display in the museum. 'The Hare' mosaic was discovered in 1971 just below the road surface during archaeological excavations in Beeches Road, on the edge of the Roman town. It had suffered little damage and, along with fragments of other mosaics from this site of an important Roman town house, was lifted for preservation and display. 'Made by local craftsmen from local stone materials, the quality of its craftsmanship sums up the care and attention which Cotswold craftsmen have given to their products over the centuries,' David says. 'The chance to be involved in that discovery, and see such a fine piece of work reappear from so long ago, leaves a strong memory. The past of this town is to me a living thing, not consigned to oblivion like so much of our history.'

from their sunnier homeland. The Romans are credited with introducing their own breed of sheep to improve the native stock, resulting in the famous Cotswold sheep that in time became the backbone of the country's economy. Along with other delicacies such as asparagus, the Romans are said to have brought to our land the stinging nettle (purportedly to 'warm up the British').

It is the mosaic pavements, excavated from what must have been the grander houses of Roman Cirencester, that epitomise the opulence of the households and the artistry of the mosaicist. Classical and mythical, symbolic and also symmetrical, these rediscovered mosaic designs and motifs - intricately composed over a millennium and a half ago and since buried under gardens, roadways and buildings - must have been stunning in their own time. Some 80 mosaic pavements have been recorded, some dating from as early as the second century. Outstanding among the rescued and re-laid pavements is one depicting 'Hunting Dogs and the Seasons', discovered in Dyer Street in 1849, and 'The Hare' mosaic excavated from Beeches Road.

The Romans laid out their town on a typical rectangular street system, little of which has survived. Nor have any temples or significant shrines been identified, despite the tolerance the Romans were known to have had regarding different beliefs, especially those of the native British Dobunni, who still worshipped pagan idols of fertility, healing and eternity. A sculptured trio of mother goddesses - the Deae Matres - with each figure holding a tray or basket of food, was unearthed during the construction of Ashcroft Road. Also, an exquisitely sculpted representation of Jupiter, a sacred cult figure of the more classically cultured Romans, was found close to the museum in which he now stands, peering through the elaborately stylised foliage of the fallen column with his immortal stony gaze.

Christianity was decreed the official religion of the Roman Empire by Emperor Constantine in AD 312, but it is generally thought to have taken a long time to effect complete conversion in its further flung corners. That is why the discovery of a possible Christian symbol - in the form of a word square incised on a piece of plaster found in Victoria Road in 1868 - exercises the mind of many experts. The words ROTAS OPERA TENET AREPO SATOR translate as: 'The sower Arepo holds the wheel carefully', but by re-arranging the letters the word Paternoster appears down and across, leaving A and O (twice) to be interpreted as Alpha and Omega (the beginning and the end). The puzzle is why, if this is a coded statement of Christian faith, was it necessary to conceal the message in such a way, at that time during the occupation of Cirencester.

To the south-west of the town, and physically separated from it by the ring road, are the impressive mounds of the Roman amphitheatre - acknowledged to be one of the best examples of its kind in Britain. Signposts direct the visitor to the site of the large oval arena with its twin entrances, where sports and public entertainment were staged on a grand scale. (Today it is best approached by way of Sheep Street and Querns Hill.) Typical of amphitheatres built in Britain, this was an earthwork structure, thought to date from the earliest period of Roman occupation. It was created as a result of the extensive quarrying for the stone used in the buildings of the town.

The echoing roar of the crowds as they goaded on their favoured beast or gladiator at the bear-baiting or wrestling contests is carried over the centuries on the winds of fancy - heard perhaps in the hum of today's traffic on the road below, or the bark of a dog excitedly chasing a thrown stick, or the laughter of children on the grassy slopes, as these sounds of today break into the silence at this ancient site. Now, it is only the slow passing of a cloud shadow that settles fleetingly on the banked auditorium where richly clad senators and civic officers and simply clothed artisans and menial folk once gathered for their entertainment. Whether the bodies found during the building of the ring road were the price paid in human terms for those gladiatorial combats on our Cotswold soil has not been proven, but is highly likely, although the amphitheatre has not yet undergone extensive excavation.

Cemeteries, as such, have been identified outside all the major gates of Roman Corinium, and accord to the law prevailing at the time for all religious cults whereby burials had to be just beyond the town limits. The programme of excavations over the past decades gives us some idea of the population of the town: Dr Alan McWhirr, the eminent archaeologist who has contributed so much to the interpretation of Cirencester in Roman times, has estimated the figure to be within

> ## Did you know?
> 
> ### The Bull Ring
> 
> *The local name for the amphitheatre is the Bull Ring, from its use in the 18th century for bull-baiting contests.*

the region of 5-10,000. The capacity of the amphitheatre has been assessed at 8-9,000.

The affluence of the early years of the fourth century left a rich legacy of life under Roman rule, discovered only a millennium and a half later but now forming the nucleus of Cirencester's fascinating heritage. Possibly it was at this vast public space, the amphitheatre, that Corinium's golden days as the second most important city of Roman Britain came to an end. The collapse of the great empire, taking the regular army away from Britain to deal with troubles elsewhere, left the civilian populace to defend the southern part of the country against the invading Saxons and Franks, as well as to maintain good standards of living, commerce, law and order. According to the Anglo-Saxon Chronicle, Roman rule ended in Britain in AD 435.

## Roman Corinium to Norman Cyrescestre

Cirencester, together with Gloucester and Bath, was taken, according to the Chronicle, in the decisive battle of Dyrham of AD 577. The old Roman city of Corinium became the new Saxon town of Cyrn Ceastre: 'Cyrn' from the River Churn and 'Ceastre' from its origins as a fort or fortified place.

There were constant wars between the different factions of the old Saxon kingdom: one legendary tale of the besieging and burning of Cirencester in 586 came from the pen of William Worcestre, who travelled widely, recording such historical events and topographical features as he could gather from local sources. Whether his account is strictly factual or part folklore is open to question, but certainly as England's first antiquary Worcestre penned the path for successive chroniclers such as Leland and Camden in later centuries. Translated from his notes (written in Latin) on his visit to Cirencester on 19 August 1480, he recorded that the place became known as 'The City of Sparrows'.

Saxon Cirencester was within the territory of the Hwicce, under Mercian domination, and remained so until the numerous small kingdoms united into the Kingdom of England in the early part of the ninth century. It would seem from archaeological evidence that the Saxons settled to the north-west of the old city of Corinium. It appears that they eschewed the grandeur and pomp of their

**NORMAN ARCH c1955** C106051

A survival of the ancient abbey.

# CIRENCESTER – *a history and celebration of the town*

## Did you know?
### The City of Sparrows

*According to William Worcestre, Cirencester became known as The City of Sparrows because a certain Africanus (who had come from Africa) set the besieged town alight by tying wildfire 'to the feet of sparrows which hys people had caught. The sparrows being suffered to go out of hand flew into the towne to lodge themselves within the nestes which they had made in stackes or corne or eaves of houses, so that the towne was thereby set on fire, and then the Brytones issuing forth fought with their enemies and were overcome and discomforted.'*

Roman predecessors, preferring to live simpler lives in single-roomed, timber-framed huts built of wattle and daub under a thatched roof. Whether by accident or design, one of the Saxon warriors found at The Barton, on the edge of Cirencester Park, had been buried in a grave that had been dug through a fine fourth-century Orpheus mosaic.

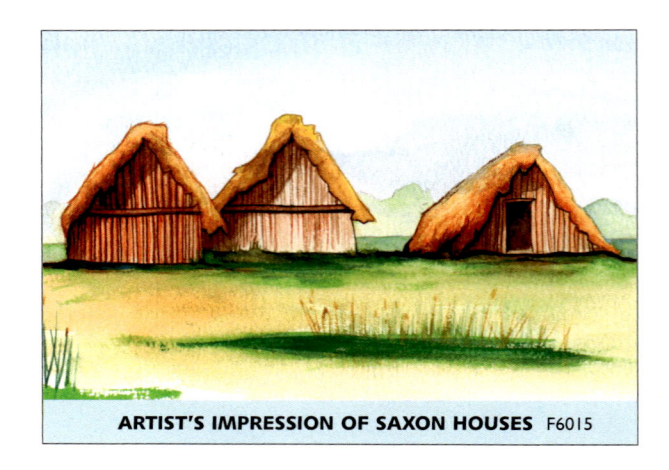

**ARTIST'S IMPRESSION OF SAXON HOUSES** F6015

**CHANTRY OF ST JOHN c1955** C106049

The remaining arches of the abbey's hospital at Spitalgate (meaning 'hospital gate').

# Roman Corinium to Norman Cyrescestre

The lifestyle of the Anglo-Saxons may have been tied more to the land of the Cotswold countryside than the paved streets of commerce, but it was perhaps because of this that Cirencester grew into the country's finest wool-producing centre. Saxon masons in Cirencester made good use of Roman stone for the foundations of their fine church, which is thought to have been built between the late seventh and the ninth century. Damaged by the Danes in one of their numerous attacks on the area, the large church was later replaced by a smaller one. Excavations have revealed that both Saxon foundations and Roman walls were utilised in the great Norman abbey, a building that was to mark the beginning of the next millennium in the town's history.

**COXWELL STREET c1960** C106116

This narrow street of mainly medieval buildings was originally called Abbot Street and renamed after a wealthy wool merchant.

Our present system of counties can be traced back to the Anglo-Saxons. A county was an administrative area comprising legal units of Hundreds; it is generally reckoned that a Hundred was made up of 100 hides (a hide being 120 acres). Although the size of a Hundred varied from place to place, it became a base unit for the purpose of taxation.

Cirencester was already a royal manor, or 'tun', by the eve of the first millennium, according to one of the scant records to survive, which reveals that Ethelred the Unready issued a charter from there in the year 999. The Anglo-Saxon Chronicle further mentions a great Council held there by King Cnut at Easter 1020. Despite the prominence of Cirencester in the county, it was Gloucester (the old Roman Glevum) that was chosen as capital of the shire. Perhaps, by no more than a whim of the monarch, at the stroke of the pen Cirencester was in Gloucestershire rather than Gloucester in Cirencestershire!

Cirencester retained its status as the centre of a Hundred, with its own court, well into the Middle Ages. Some estimate of the size of the town, which parts were owned by whom, how the land was managed and its worth, can be gleaned from the Domesday survey. In brief, the royal manor of Cirencester was recorded as comprising five hides, together with the manor of Minety. It had woods and meadows worth 5 shillings and three mills valued at 30 shillings. In the reign of Edward the Confessor (the period to which the survey related), it was his queen who received the wool from the manor sheep (the only reference to wool in the whole of the county's survey, which points to its

**CASTLE STREET c1965** C106063

Looking towards the church.

**CASTLE STREET c1965** C106112

The view from the supposed site of the Norman castle.

significance as a valuable commodity at that time). The annual rent then was £9 5s for the manor, together with grain and honey and 3,000 loaves for the royal hunting dogs! The Normans preferred money to kind, and the dogs' share was commuted to a payment of 16 shillings.

William I granted the manor of Cirencester to William Fitz Osbern, whom he created Earl of Hereford. It then passed to his son, but he fell out of royal favour following his rebellion in 1075, and, not surprisingly, the manor reverted to the Crown.

It is from the famous Domesday survey that we find the first mention of a market at Cirencester. Whether it had been in existence for very long before the Norman Conquest is not known, but the entry shows that the annual tolls raised amounted to 20 shillings. And it is as a market town that Cirencester developed over the next millennium.

**A NORMAN SHIP** F6019

24 CIRENCESTER – *a history and celebration of the town*

**THE TOWN HALL 1898** 40966

Roman Corinium to Norman Cyrescestre 25

It was built around 1500 as a business centre for the abbey, but after the Reformation was used also for meetings on town and parish church affairs.

**SOUTH PORCH 1902** 48822

The beautiful fan-vaulted ceiling of the ground floor of the old abbey's Town Hall makes a stunning entrance to the church of St John the Baptist.

CHAPTER TWO

## Medieval Monopolies to Georgian Grace and Favours

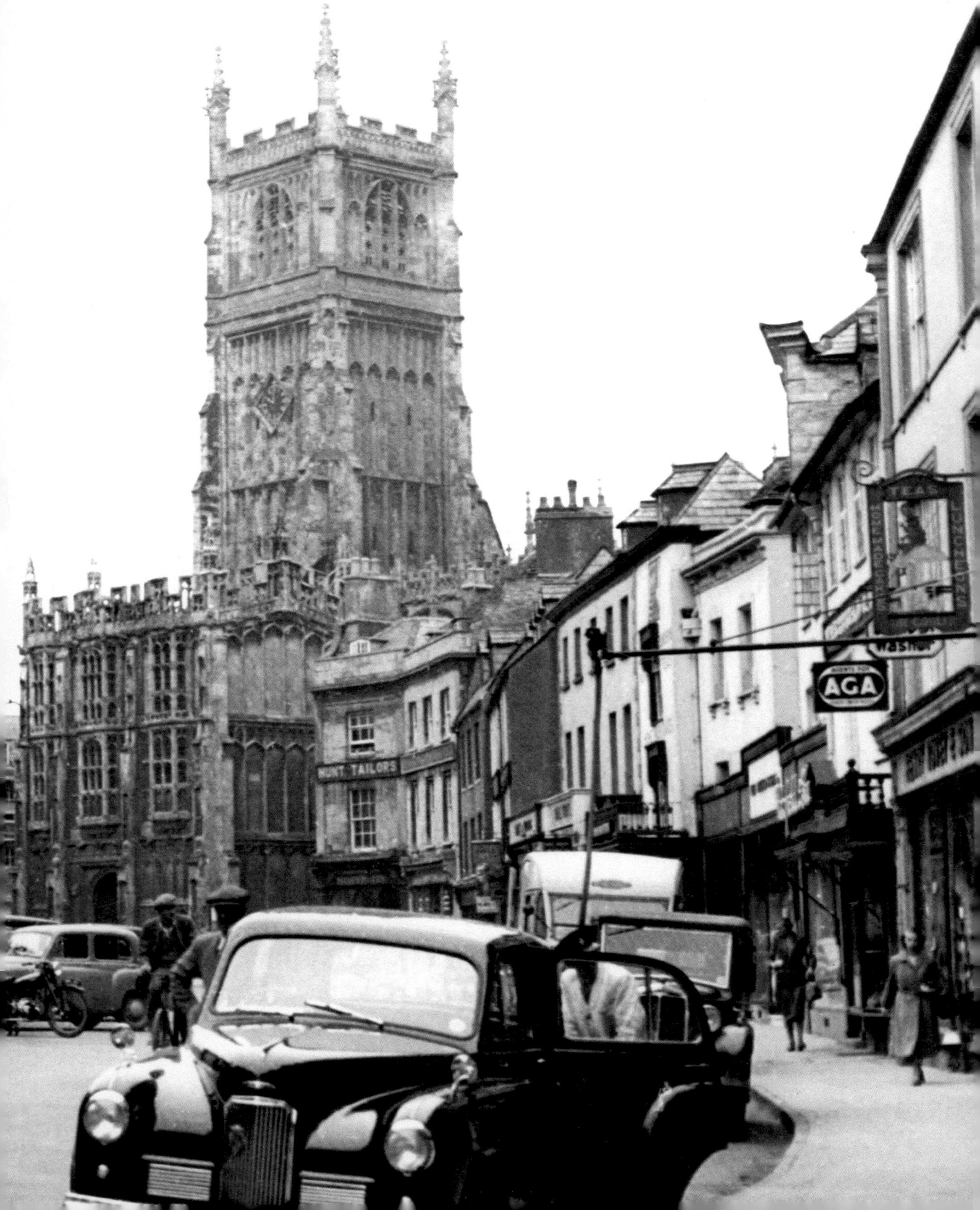
HUNT TAILORS
AGA

# CIRENCESTER – *a history and celebration of the town*

BY THE time William I gave his 'deep speech' at Gloucester (resulting in the great Domesday survey), the Cotswolds in general, and the Cirencester area in particular, had been turned into a well-cultivated rural region by some 15 or 16 generations of farming Anglo-Saxons. William must have been mightily pleased with Cirencester, since its 'new market' was by then an important trading centre. Although records are not consistent in confirming whether the town was a 'borough' or a 'vill', because it was a manor of royal demesne it was obviously advantageous to accord the tenants the status of burgesses when it came to paying royal tallage (or tax).

The Saxons may have been sons of the soil when it came to the making of the landscape, but it was the Normans who dug deeper for the honey-coloured limestone to raise a townscape in a dominant design, as had preceding conquerors seven centuries before. The Normans did so in their own style - masterful and meaningful, without ever replicating the opulence of the Romans - stamping their identity on the country that was to become their homeland, not just an outpost of a vast empire. Quite literally, they laid the foundations on which successive builders created the vernacular style that has become synonymous with the Cotswolds. Man worked with nature, using the stone of

**CASTLE STREET FROM SILVER STREET c1965** C106129

The 'Black Horse', claimed to be the oldest pub in the town, dates back to the 15th century. The black horse depicted on the sign has changed over the years from a heavy cart horse to a sleek polo pony.

the land and pitching the angles and form of the buildings to meet the demands of the environment. Cotswold architecture grew organically, rooted in the very land from which it was born; it has become a homogenous whole - blending in and becoming part of the very landscape itself.

Only a couple of documents mention that Cirencester had a castle, in the manner of Norman defence plans. During the civil war between Stephen and Matilda, a contemporary chronicler recorded that Stephen, after taking Cirencester by surprise 'gave it to the flames and razed to the ground the rampart and the outworks'. And William Worcestre, writing in the reign of Edward IV about historical facts he had gleaned on his travels, stated 'Grimond's Castle is another castle in Cirencester where King Arthur was crowned near the Chapel of St Cecilia's the Virgin, on the opposite, west, side of the town'. Whether this is a fact or just another fanciful fable of the Arthurian legend set in the Cotswolds is anyone's guess. Serious historical studies have reckoned the site of the vanished castle is somewhere in the area of the present mansion in Cirencester Park. Cecily Hill, which leads to the park, was known at one time as St Cecilia's Street. Other echoes from that long ago era are retained in the name of Castle Street, which runs from the park perimeter to the Market Place. The street now known as Park Lane was once called Law Ditch, which could be a reference to the moat that would have surrounded the castle. The castle was not included in the township and was a self-governing entity.

**THE 'BLACK HORSE' 2004** C106704k (June Lewis-Jones)

In 2004 there is no horse on the sign, only the name.

More prominent in stature and dominant over both the townscape and the townsfolk was the great abbey of St Mary, the biggest of the five Augustinian houses founded by Henry I. Consecrated in 1130, and endowed with valuable lands by the king and a third of the market tolls that had belonged to the parish church at the time of the Conquest, the abbey became more powerful as its riches increased. The Augustinian Order was much favoured by Henry I, but he expressly reserved his hunting rights and the 'making of assarts' (clearing woodland) when he gave the monks Oakley Wood. The abbey church overlapped the site of the pre-Conquest parish church, which was finally demolished to construct the abbey nave. Building of the present parish church of St John the Baptist is thought to have started about 1120, which suggests that it and the building of the abbey of St Mary may have proceeded concurrently. It is interesting to trace the two 12th-century arches (one of which is now an internal doorway leading from St Catherine's Chapel to the Lady Chapel) that once served the monks as an external entrance, through the north wall of the chancel arch of the parish church to the neighbouring abbey.

When the abbey's own church was dedicated with great pomp and ceremony in 1176, it was Henry II who attended, with no fewer than four bishops. Henry II, like his grandfather, Henry I, also favoured Cirencester abbey, granting it the revenues of the township. Thirteen years later, when Richard I was on the throne, he granted the abbey the manorial rights in perpetuity, as well as the lordship of the Seven Hundreds. This was an area that extended eastwards from the Leach Valley to the Wiltshire Avon westwards, with the developing market towns of Fairford and Tetbury and the lucrative wool trade from the vast sheepwalks on the rolling Cotswolds between, all contributing to the abbey's coffers.

The parish church of St John the Baptist was literally overshadowed by the abbey church of St Mary, and the abbey itself was a strong statement in stone of a seat of monastic power. Successive monarchs, in return for money to finance their own royal projects, strengthened the abbot's control. A succession of royals, from the first three Henrys to the first three Edwards, visited, sojourned, held court or spent Christmas at Cirencester as guests of the abbot. As feudal lord, the abbot had absolute authority over his manorial tenants, and his rights were jealously guarded. Disputes, fines, penalties and punishments meted out in his name included the ducking of mischief makers on the 'gongstool' (from which comes the name of the Gunstool brook); the public abuse, attack and humiliation of being held

**JOUSTING KNIGHTS** F6017

## Medieval Monopolies to Georgian Grace and Favours

The shops depicted include Stevens (on the left) and Smith the Druggist (in the centre with Pickwickian windows).

in the stocks and pillory that stood in the Market Place; and the confiscation of a felon's goods if he was hanged. On one occasion the abbot lent his gallows to cronies in the next parish, but woe betide any manor within the Hundred that set up its own gallows and deprived the abbot of his dues.

Customary tenants of Cirencester abbey, who held land in return for service, worked on its three farms - The Barton, Almery Grange and the Spyringate Grange - the last two being within the abbey precinct. The Barton's circular dovecote and great barn can still be seen today from one of the walkways branching to the right in Cirencester Park. In addition to doing compulsory service, these tenants were subject to a number of levies. They could not sell or bequeath their land without the abbot's permission, and if this was granted, the heir had to pay a fine, or heriot, in the form of his best horse or beast. On the tenant's death the second best chattel was due to the church as 'mortuary', but that went to the abbot because he was also rector of the parish church. And if a tenant's daughter married, the abbot levied another fine, called merchet. Also, the tenant's corn had to be ground at the abbey mills, which by the end of the 13th century were the three listed as belonging to Cirencester manor at Domesday: Brain's Mill at the Gildenbridge in Gloucester Street and both of the Barton Mills. Tenants also had to pay a 'chepingavel' (tax) to the abbot for the right to buy and sell goods (except horses) at the weekly market.

Generations of Cirencester townsfolk tried to break free of the oppression of the abbey, and Petitions and Inquisitions punctuate the pages of the town's medieval history, but each time the abbot of the day was either granted indemnity or pardoned. Allegations against the abbey included its appropriation of both St John's Hospital in Spitalgate Lane (whose arches remain as an architectural feature in later buildings) and St Lawrence Hospital (built as a leper house on the corner of Gloucester Street and Barton Lane and converted by Abbot Hereward in the 14th century to almshouses for two women).

> **Did you know?**
>
> **The Almshouses**
>
> Rebuilt about 1800, the almshouses are on the site of the original medieval hospital.

A petition to Edward III in 1343 listed several grievances, including the hunting to extinction of the deer in Oakley Forest, enclosure of common land at the Querns and, most significantly, encroachment upon His Majesty's highway by building what developed into three streets at the top of the Market Place. The clearance of the huddle of these narrow streets, with buildings almost touching the parish church, was not carried out until the early 19th century. The battle for borough status - which the townsmen insisted was conferred on them by ancient deed (which, conveniently, the abbey could not produce) - made its periodical appearance, but it was not until 1571 that parliamentary borough status was granted, though the powers of self-government were limited.

The abbey's stranglehold on the life and trade of the town was further strengthened in 1379 when the Pope raised Abbot Nicholas to the status of bishop. Cirencester then became a mitred abbey. It was the rebellious earls of Kent and Salisbury who inadvertently helped to free the inhabitants of stifling monastic power in 1400. Arriving to muster support for their rebellion against Henry IV, the noble renegades encountered unexpected opposition in the town and put it to the torch in an attempt to subjugate the townsfolk. Taking the law into their own hands, the men of Cirencester imprisoned their captives in the abbey gaol, brought them out the following day and beheaded them publicly in the Market Place.

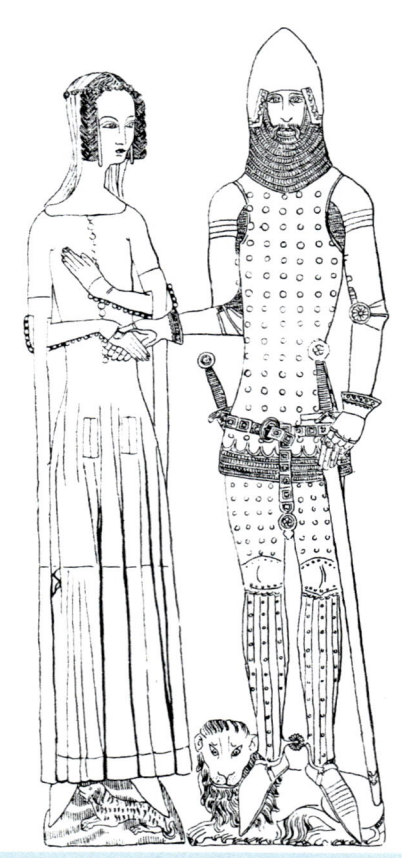

**A MEDIEVAL KNIGHT AND HIS LADY FROM A TOMB IN INGHAM CHURCH, NORFOLK** F6018

## Medieval Monopolies to Georgian Grace and Favours

> ### Did you know?
> ### The Townsfolk Fight Back
>
> Shakespeare famously dramatised the torching of the town and the townspeople's subsequent beheading of the earls in 'Richard II', Act V:
>
> 'Kind Uncle York the latest news we hear
> Is that the rebels have consumed with fire
> Our town of Cicester in Gloucestershire.
> The next news is, I have to London sent
> The heads of Salisbury, Spencer, Blunt and Kent'.
>
> Henry IV was mightily pleased with this gift of rebellious heads and reciprocated by allowing the townsfolk to keep the treasure chests that the earls had brought with them on their recruiting campaign. The town bailiff received an annual pension of 100 marks, and an annual grant of venison and wine was made from the royal preserves:
>
> 'For the men: four does in season out of his forest of Bredon and one hogshead of wine out of his port of Bristol. For the women: six bucks in right season and one hogshead of wine out of the same port.'

For the first time it was the town rather than the abbey that was in royal favour, and the townsfolk pressed on with their campaign for independence from the abbey's control. It took two years and strong resolve before obligatory service on the abbey lands was withdrawn and control of the town's trade was achieved through the granting of a guild merchant. A decade later, under the new monarch, Henry V, the abbey regained control and the guild charter was repealed.

Three Henrys later the old order changed for good. Under Henry VIII's dissolution of the monasteries, Cirencester Abbey, assessed as the wealthiest of nearly 200 Augustinian houses in the kingdom, fell. Six days before Christmas in 1539, the last abbot signed an admission of the king's supremacy. The great abbey closed its doors forever on the last day of that year, bringing to an end the chapter covering some four centuries of the town's history.

**ARTIST'S IMPRESSION OF JANE SEYMOUR, THIRD WIFE OF HENRY VIII** F6023

# The Abbey Grounds

The abbey grounds, with the river, lake and expansive grassed areas, afford an attractive pastoral oasis within a few minutes' walk of the bustling town centre. To the right of the scene in photograph C106705k are the outlines of the old Roman city walls. In the far distance, to the right of the church, are Abbey House flats. These replaced the Abbey House mansion, which in turn had replaced the ancient Augustinian abbey.

Towards the parish church, the site of the destroyed abbey church of St Mary is marked by stones set in the grass (see photograph C106706k). Close by are an informative map and plan interpreting the location and dimensions of the former abbey. On the left in the photograph and lying within the former cloister, is a curved stone balustrade bounding the terrace of Abbey House flats. Signposts direct the visitor to other points of interest such as the Norman Arch and the Roman walls.

**ABBEY GROUNDS 2004** C106705k *(June Lewis-Jones)*

**SITE OF ABBEY CHURCH OF ST MARY 2004** C106706k *(June Lewis-Jones)*

## Medieval Monopolies to Georgian Grace and Favours

Few could have mourned the passing of those repressive times. The people were free at last to live their own lives and trade as other market towns did. There was fine stone to be salvaged from the razed main abbey and its church, though other buildings deemed suitable for secular use were retained.

Here and there throughout the town there is evidence of ancient carvings and stonework that had once been part of the great abbey - a number of stone plinths can be found fronting houses, as at numbers 33 and 35 in Gloucester Street.

**GLOUCESTER STREET 1898** 42362

Number 29 was the 18th-century theatre.

The only building to survive in its entirety from that repressive period is the 12th-century Gate House, generally called the Norman Arch, in Spitalgate, so named because it was the entrance to the abbey's Hospitium. The Gate House was presented to the town in 1964 as a memorial to Col W A Chester-Master, whose family had inherited the old abbey property and lands through Dr Richard Master, physician to Elizabeth I. He paid the Queen £590 16s 3d for the abbey site. As a further mark of gratitude to her physician, Elizabeth Tudor made him a personal present of the silver gilt

**GLOUCESTER STREET c1950** C106019

This street scene has changed little since photograph 42362 (facing page) was taken, over half a century ago.

cup that had belonged to her mother, the ill-fated Anne Boleyn. He later bequeathed this cup to the parish church, where it can be seen today in its special glass case.

It is the church of St John the Baptist that stands as stony sentinel to the resurgence of Cirencester as capital of the Cotswolds. Emerging at last from the oppressive shadow of the abbey, the townspeople concentrated on enlarging and beautifying their own parish church. The spoils from the executed earls bestowed on them by Henry IV funded the building of the church tower. Ambitious plans for topping it with a spire had to be curtailed when it was discovered that the foundations of the 12th-century church in Gosditch Street had been laid on an old Roman ditch and were prone to flooding.

# Medieval Monopolies to Georgian Grace and Favours

**PRINT OF OLD GOSDITCH STREET 1804** ZZZ00391

To counteract the effects that consequent subsidence would have caused, and to help balance the weight of the already soaring tower, huge stone buttresses were added as support, both inside and out. The flying buttresses are now regarded as a special architectural feature.

A legacy of the monastic dynasty is the church's magnificent south porch, with its finely fenestrated detail giving it a fairytale castle look. Built for the abbey in around 1500 in the Perpendicular style with an exquisite fan-vaulted ceiling, it makes a grand entrance to the church, but was in fact designed as a kind of civil court room where business and legal transactions were carried out. Following the dissolution, the chamber above the porch became the Town Hall, and transferred to the care of the church in 1672. Somewhat weatherworn, but still discernable, are the interesting figures on the outside of the porch 'pourtraying the social life and customs of three or four centuries since'.

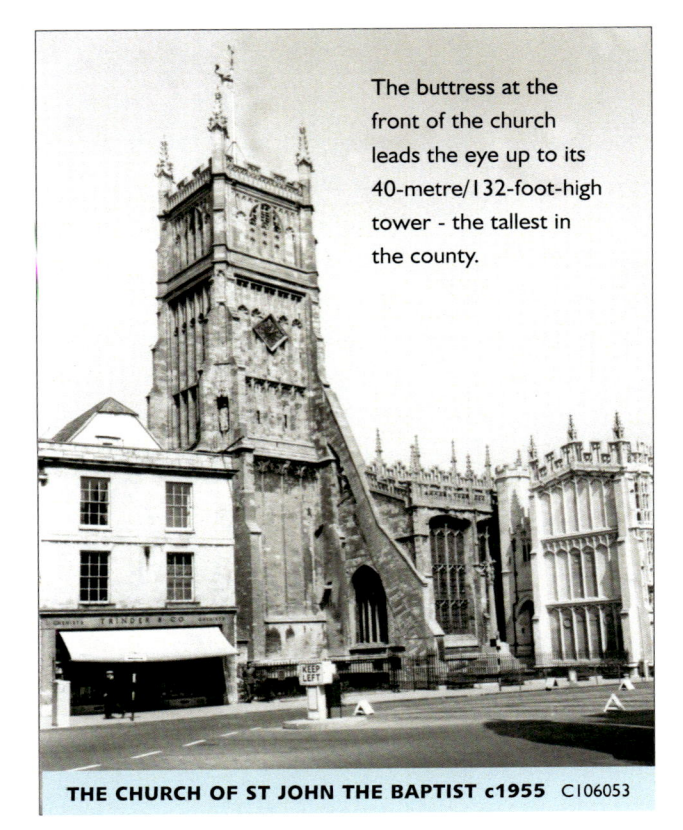

The buttress at the front of the church leads the eye up to its 40-metre/132-foot-high tower - the tallest in the county.

**THE CHURCH OF ST JOHN THE BAPTIST c1955** C106053

The Middle Ages have been termed the Age of the Golden Fleece, and a medieval Italian merchant, Francesco Datini, is quoted as recording that 'The finest and most expensive wool was the English which came from the Chondisgualdo [Cotswolds] and in particular from Northleccio [Northleach] and the great Abbey lands of Sirencestri [Cirencester]'. This could possibly have been the source of the well-known jingle: 'In Europe the best wool is English; In England the best wool is Cotswold'.

In acknowledgement of the fact that England's wealth at the time was to be found on the backs of sheep, the Chancellor of the Exchequer, mightily pleased with the revenues from exported woollen cloth, plumped himself down on a sack of wool - and the Woolsack became, and still is, the symbolic seat of the nation's financial power. Now, however, it is stuffed with wool from the four countries of the United Kingdom rather than solely that of the native Cotswold breed. These animals have an extraordinary heavy fleece, ruffed round their necks (giving rise to their long-standing name of Cotswold Lions), and their slightly aquiline faces suggest a distinctive Roman ancestry. Cirencester, at the centre of the wool trade, attracted a number of the country's richest merchants. They endowed the church with funds for the rebuilding of the nave by the mid 16th century, creating the largest parish church in the whole of Gloucestershire - and often referred to as the Cathedral of the Cotswolds. Their memorial brasses in the church give some idea of their dress at the time. (Brass rubbing has become an extremely popular activity here, with the church shop stocking the appropriate materials.)

Freed from the monastic monopoly on the wool market, the 'woolmen' became the new masters. An analysis of the trades and occupations in the town in 1608 - based on the men deemed 'able bodied' (simply on account of being between 20 and 60 years of age and mustered for possible service in the county's militia) - recorded some 18 per cent involved directly in the manufacturing of woollen cloth. Just as the ghosts of the abbey's past linger in the names of the roads and streets of Cirencester today, the once-so-important wool threads through the town's fabric in names such as Dyer Street, Sheep Street, the Fleece Hotel and the Woolmarket. The latter is a pedestrian-only shopping centre, attractively set around an extended courtyard linking the Market Place from Dyer Street to the Waterloo car park, from which the abbey grounds can be reached. A model of a ram with curly horns (so not modelled on the authentic hornless Cotswold breed) symbolises the name of the precinct.

*Medieval Monopolies to Georgian Grace and Favours*

**THE FLEECE HOTEL IN DYER STREET c1955** C106065

**THE RAM 2004** C106707k (June Lewis-Jones)

A curly horned ram makes an apt centrepiece to the courtyard shopping area of the Woolmarket.

# Evolution of the Town Centre

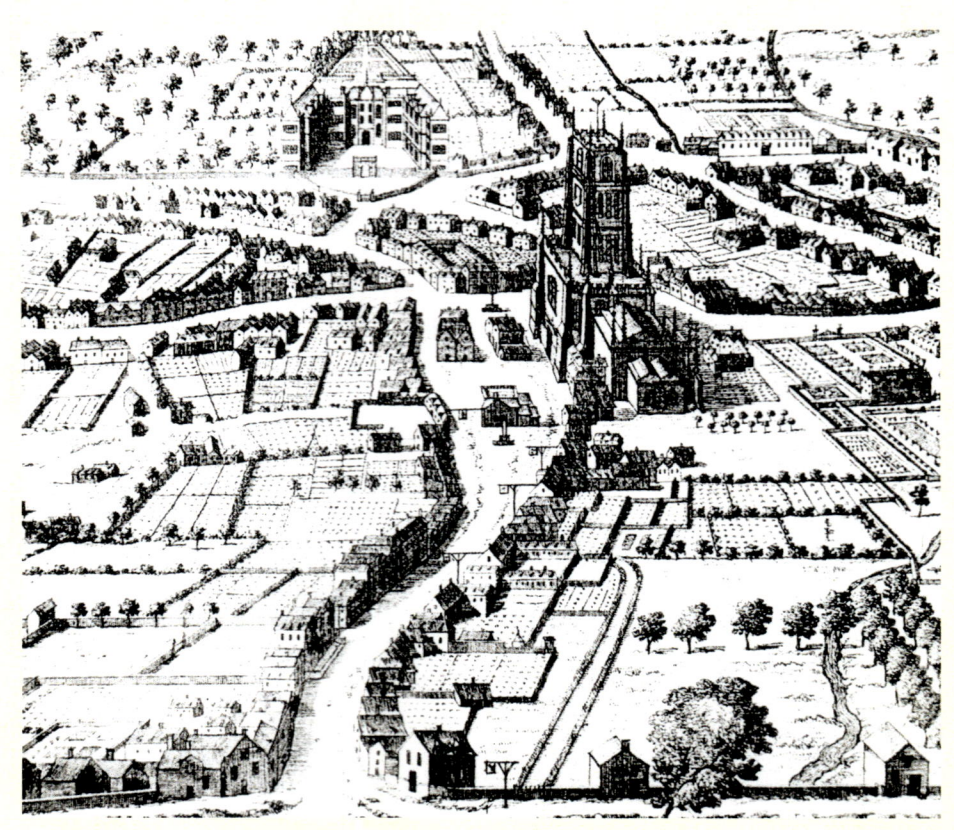

**CIRENCESTER 1700** ZZZ00390

The picture ZZZ00390 shows the well-planned market town of Cirencester in 1700, as seen through an artist's eye. There is a clutch of ancient small streets in the Market Place in front of the church, with a Market Cross at each end. At the top of the picture is Cirencester Mansion House, fronting the landscaped park, and to the right of the church are the abbey house and grounds, home of the Chester-Master family.

In the engraving (ZZZ00389) the Shambles looks picturesque, with a huddle of small streets in close proximity within the Market Place, but this idyllic scene was probably far removed from reality.

The ancient buildings had been cleared away by 1830, leaving the spacious Market Place we know today. The nearby Woolmarket in Dyer Street is now an attractive precinct of specialist shops.

# Medieval Monopolies to Georgian Grace and Favours

**WOOLMARKET, DYER STREET 2004**
C106708k *(June Lewis-Jones)*

**ENGRAVING OF THE SHAMBLES** ZZZ00389

Coxwell Street, a couple of streets to the north of Castle Street, is a delight. This narrow ribbon of a street is as near perfect an example of 'genuine old Cotswold' as can be found anywhere. It was around much earlier than the wealthy Elizabethan wool merchant, John Coxwell, after whom it was named; for nearly half a millennium it was known as 'abbotstrete' or Abbot's Street, reflecting its original ownership. No doubt much of the surplus stone from the demolished abbey went into the building of most of the town's houses and cottages, many of which have changed little over the last 300 years. Woolgatherers (formerly Coxwell Court, now tastefully up-dated), embracing a cluster of buildings from wool lofts to the counting house, marks a historical cornerstone of this fascinating street. The front door to the family home is in Coxwell Street. On the other side is Thomas Street, from where it is not too difficult to imagine a scene with horse-drawn carts overflowing with cream fleeces creaking their way through the archway into the courtyard of a wool warehouse.

It is in Thomas Street that we find the oldest secular building in Cirencester, Weavers' Hall - originally an almshouse for four poor weavers, and known as St Thomas' Hospital, from which the street takes its name. It was founded by the bequest of Sir William Nottingham, a local man from a family of established clothiers, who rose to eminence as Attorney General to Edward IV. Trusteeship of the almshouse was vested in the Cirencester Weavers' Company, which was already well established when Sir William made his will in

**CASTLE STREET c1950** C106046

A number of the finest town houses were built for the wool merchants. The building on the corner of Silver Street and Castle Street (now Lloyds Bank), was described by the late David Verey, the eminent architectural historian, as 'the best example of Palladian architecture in Cirencester'.

1483. A charter granted by Philip and Mary, dated 18 May 1558, refers to the Company of the 'Customes and Constitutions of olde antiquitie out of tyme and mynde belonging to the Crafte and occupacion of Weavers in the Towne of Cisceter'. Elizabeth I confirmed the charter in 1566, when it was ruled that 'two of the most discreatist and wisest men of the mysterie of weavers' should be elected as wardens at the annual meeting to be held on St Katheryne's Eve. The Weavers' Company regulated the trade, preventing any unauthorised setting up 'of lombes' (looms), and acted as watchdog over the training of apprentices. The company is still in existence, although its remit has changed with the times, as have the tenancy rules for today's families who live in this ancient building.

The Civil War brought battle and bloodshed to the streets of the quiet market town. 'The Taking of Cicester in the County of Glocester on Thursday, February 2, 1642, by 7000 of the Cavaliers, under the command of Prince Rupert ... and divers others' - to quote the cover of a contemporary pamphlet - has been extremely well documented. The pamphlet was sent 'to a friend in London, by one who was present at, and some dayes after the

*Medieval Monopolies to Georgian Grace and Favours* 43

## Charity Schools

**FIGURE OF A BLUECOAT BOY**
**c1965** C106097

This 18th-century painted figure is in the nave by the south door - originally it stood in the porch begging for donations to the schools.

**DOLLS IN SCHOOL UNIFORM**
ZZZ00388 *(June Lewis-Jones)*

School uniform originated in the charity schools, where distinctive clothing for pupils formed part of the benefaction. Many schools therefore became known by the colour of the pupils' coats. The models here display the style of dress worn by the early pupils of Powell's Schools: Cirencester Blue School was endowed by Thomas Powell in 1714, originally for half days only so that the rest of the day could be spent in 'profitable labour for their parents at home'. The expenses records show that the pupils wrote their way through some 8,200 quills in the first ten years at a cost of £2 4s. In addition to their clothing they received free hair cuts, for which one Aaron Sparrow had the contract, worth 2s a year. The Yellow School was founded by Thomas Powell's widow, Rebecca, and opened in 1740. As well as basic education, these schools were an early form of apprenticeship, with the boys being taught the craft of stocking weaving and the girls spinning.

taking of it, published because of the many false reports that were in Print concerning that businesse'.

One of the county's foremost chroniclers of that event was John Corbet, a Gloucestershire man who was a Bachelor of Magdalen College,

Oxford, at the age of 16 and became chaplain to the governor of Gloucester, Colonel Edward Massey, who figured large in the Civil War. Corbet's account of the fighting may appear quaint today, but there is nothing comical about the horror of slaughter by sword or shot, or the terror experienced by those who witnessed the reality of war in their own streets, where 'the passages were many and open, and the enemy soone came upon their backes, as for the country-men, their houre was not yet come, neither had they quitted such imployment as did infeeble their spirits, not entered the schoole of war to study

**THE MARKET PLACE c1955** C106038

The King's Head Hotel (on the left with canopied entrance) is reputed to be haunted by a Royalist. On the far left is the Corn Hall.

## Medieval Monopolies to Georgian Grace and Favours

indignation, revenge and bloud, that alone can overcome the terrour of an army'.

In a desperate attempt at some form of defence, the townsmen barricaded the front of their church with hundreds of bales of wool -in much the same way as the town's vulnerable buildings were sandbagged during the Second World War. But wool was still a valuable commodity, and became one of the spoils of the war along with money, livestock and food. There was indiscriminate looting and ransacking of houses - even Royalist sympathisers had their houses ransacked. John Plot found his house in Coxwell Street 'full of soldiers and £1,200 taken', which is a measure of the wealth of some individuals at the time. His house, number 10, still bears his initials on the door jamb, and the date it was built. There was brave resistance to the invasion by those who Corbet described as not trained for warfare. An epitaph to a local clothier who fell with the colours in his hand can be found on the south aisle of the parish church, containing these lines: 'He looseing quiet by warre yet gained his ease by it/PAINE's life began and paine did cease.' And thus Hodgkinson Paine is accorded recognition, albeit in a pun on his name, in the taking of Cirencester. He was just one of many townsfolk who, according to Corbet 'were at their wits end, and stood like men amazed, feare bereft them of understanding and memory, begat confusion in the minde within, and the thronging thoughts did oppresse and stop the course of action …'

> Founded with a capital of £3,000, the Corn Hall was built in the early 1860s in an Italianate style as a marketing centre for the corn trade. It replaced the medieval Boothall medley of stalls and was the forum for the Hiring (old Statute) Fair, when agricultural and domestic workers put themselves forward for employment.

**PRINT OF THE NORTH PORCH OF THE CHURCH** ZZZ00386

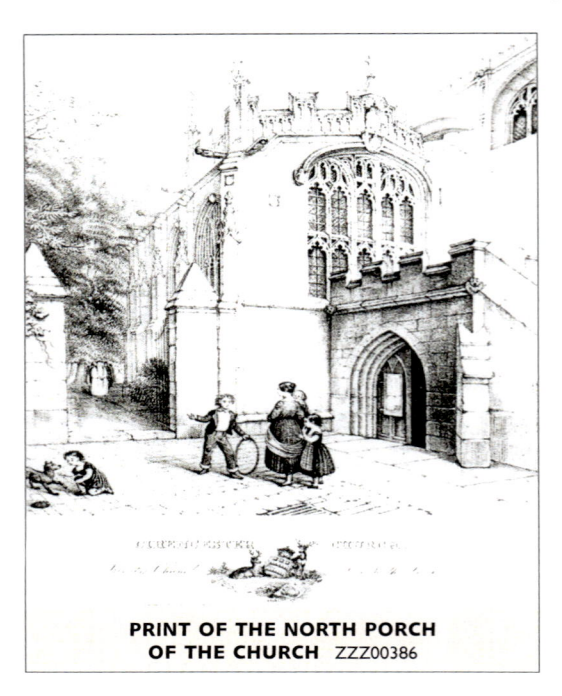

The ancient Market Cross now stands where the children are.

this month'. Eleven years later the bells of St John's, silenced under Cromwell's rule, rang out again when the monarchy was restored and Charles II entered his capital on 29 May.

Except for the duration of the war years, the bells of St John the Baptist Church have been rung each year to commemorate the Restoration of the Monarchy. The Pardoe Legacy pays a small amount for the bells to be rung between 6 and 6.30am on Oak Apple Day (29 May). Cirencester was the first town in the county to have a peal of 12 bells. Peter Holden, the Tower Captain, says that 'they used to claim to be the oldest in the world, but this is contentious; but it is probably true to say that Cirencester has had a peal of twelve bells for the longest continuous period. Several bells have been recast over the years, one as recently as 1984.'

Historians estimate some 300 defendants were killed and 1,200 captured and locked in the parish church all night. Distraught families gathered outside and broke some of the windows in order to get food and water to the prisoners. No doubt their kinsfolk lined the streets to watch as men were driven like cattle towards Oxford. They were, as one man described, 'without stockings on our legs, or shooes on our feet, or hats on our heads, many of us having no Dublets, and some Gentlemen of good quality without Breeches'. They eventually returned home after making an 'abject submission to the King', whose execution in 1649 prompted the vicar of Cirencester to write in the parish register: 'O, England, what did'st thou do, the 30th of

**PRINT OF OLD CIRENCESTER** ZZZ00385

Street sellers add to this picturesque scene of Old Cirencester.

## Medieval Monopolies to Georgian Grace and Favours

The social structure of the country changed dramatically in the aftermath of the Civil War. By the accession of the first King George in 1714, power was sought through political influence and patronage, and the landed gentry became the new masters, philanthropists and employers on a grand scale. They set about founding and improving their manorial estates, with Cirencester still 'full of clothiers and driving a great trade in wool', according to Daniel Defoe writing in 1724. But by the time George II was on the throne (1727), the wool trade was on the decline. Cirencester was still a market centre, but what was attracting business to the town was corn and dairy produce and the expanding range of goods dealt with through a new generation of entrepreneurs, bankers, and professional people in law, medicine and education. The increase in and diversity of trade expanded as road transport developed and coaching inns sprang up to accommodate travellers and horses. By the end of the 18th century the journey to London that had previously taken three days was accomplished in one, in the Cirencester 'Flying Machine' - but only in summer, when it could 'fly' along the turnpike and toll roads.

News from the outside world was relayed to the country town by way of the 'Cirencester Flying Post'. Brought out in 1718 it was one of the earliest local newspapers in the kingdom, but published little of what was going on in the locality. It was Samuel Rudder - a writer as well as a printer, with a shop in Dyer Street - who published what

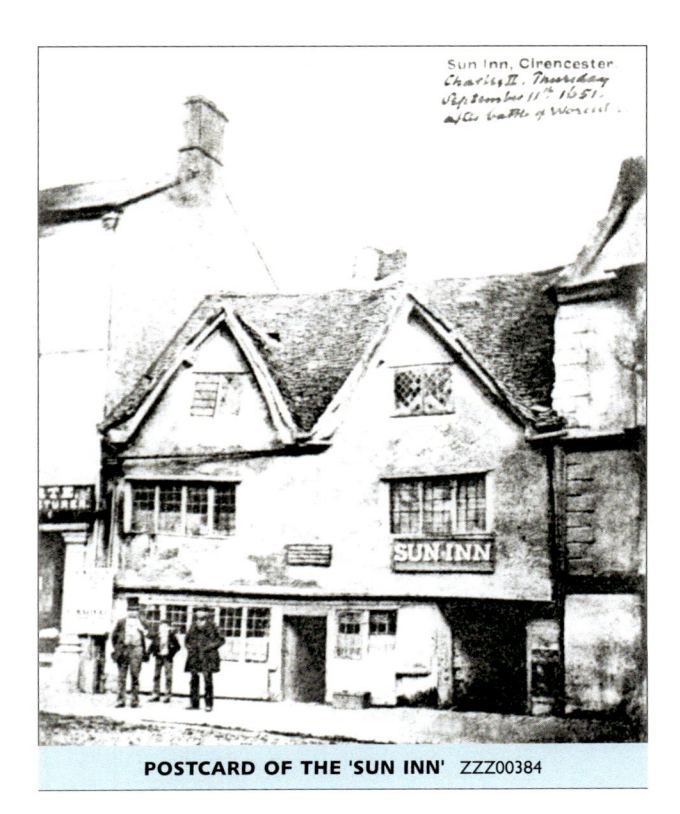

**POSTCARD OF THE 'SUN INN'** ZZZ00384

A handwritten note on the card states: 'Charles II. Thursday, September 11th 1651, after the Battle of Worcester'. This probably implies that it was at this 17th-century inn that the fugitive king sought refuge - as legend has it, dressed as a farm labourer.

has been regarded as a revision of the county history by Sir Robert Atkyns, and a valuable contemporary record of Cirencester.

Influential during a century of Georgian grace and favour were the two principal estates of Cirencester Park and the abbey grounds and farms (under the Bathurst and Master families, respectively). As well as being powerful and philanthropic in the local area, they also had political power, for they shared control of the two Parliamentary seats for most of the 18th century.

48  CIRENCESTER – *a history and celebration of the town*

**DYER STREET c1955**  C106036

By the 1920s the Grove Garage had replaced the 'Sun Inn' (see photograph ZZZ00384).

**COACHING PRINT**  F6021

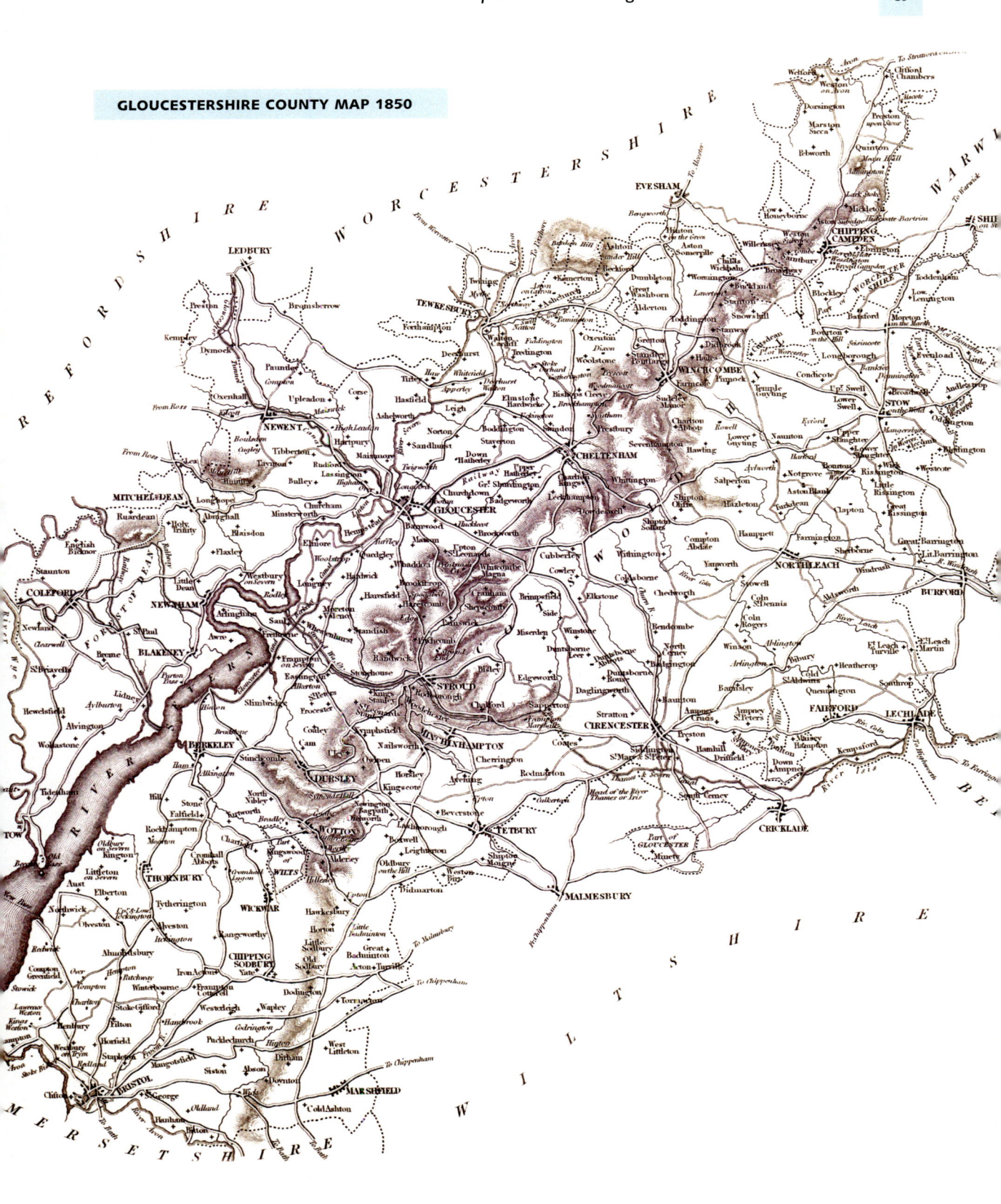

## Medieval Monopolies to Georgian Grace and Favours

**GLOUCESTERSHIRE COUNTY MAP 1850**

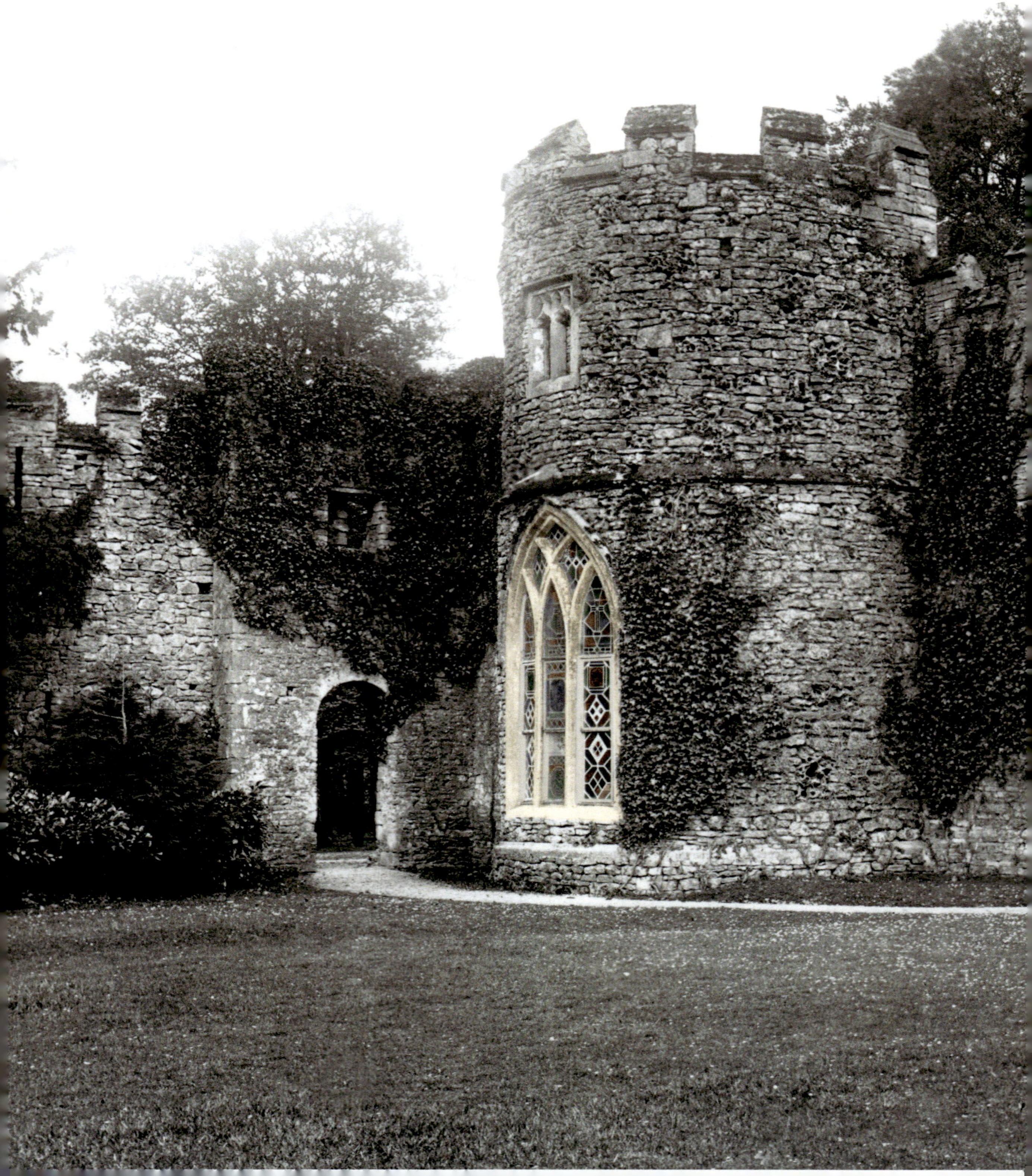

CHAPTER THREE

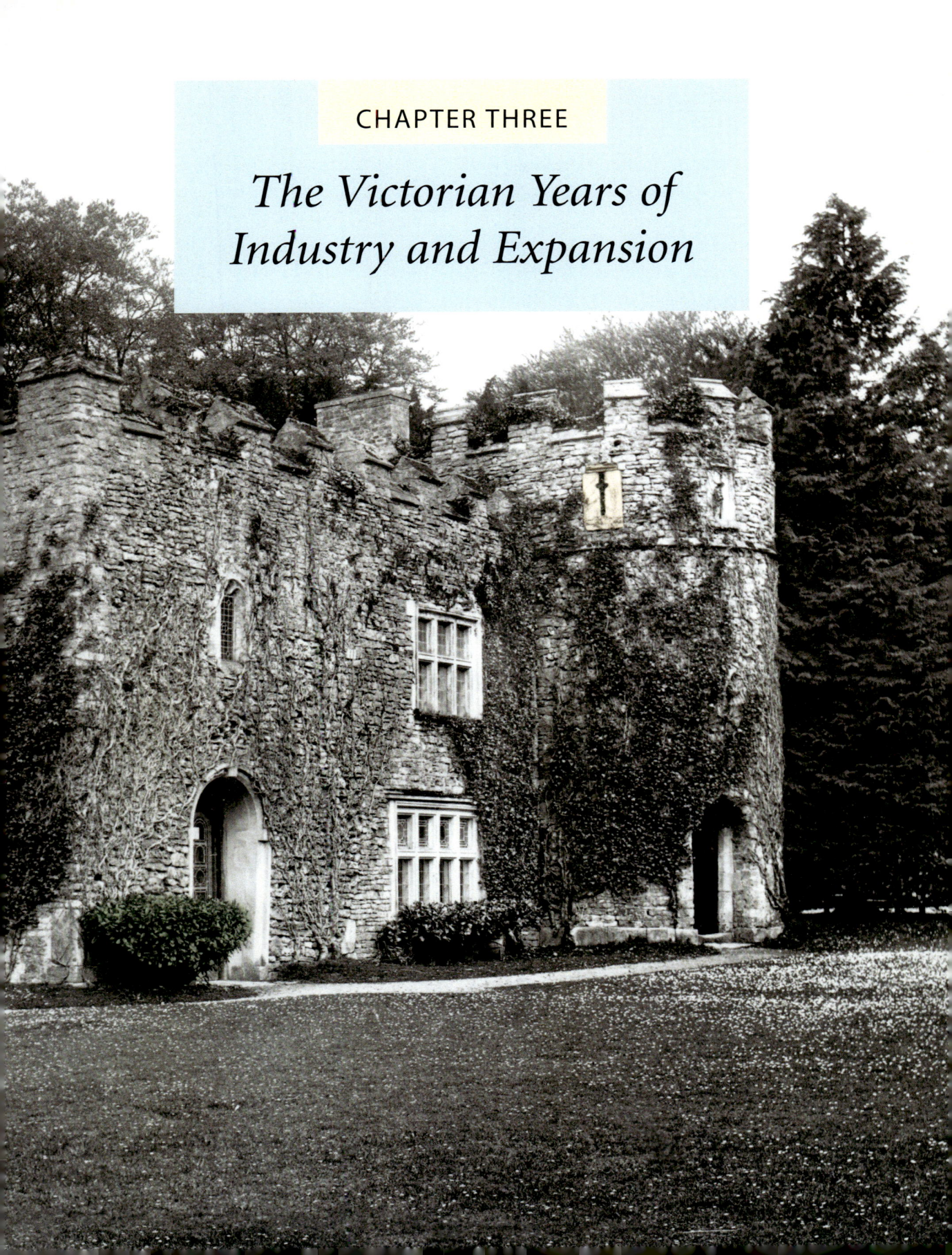

## *The Victorian Years of Industry and Expansion*

THERE IS a tale of one old lady who, when asked for whom she was going to vote in an election, replied: 'I won't be voting Unionist, I don't approve of Unions, I was born and bred in the Workhouse; I can't be Liberal 'cos I've got nothing to give; and I shan't be voting Socialist - I don't hold with them Socials, the rooms get that hot'!

Little would this lady have ever thought that her reckoning of the political parties would be of such interest that it would appear in print in 'The Gloucestershire Countryside', 'The official organ of the Gloucestershire branch of the Council for the Preservation of Rural England'. But quaint as her logic appeared even then - in the early 1930s - it illustrates how her reasoning in her old age was coloured by her early years in Victorian England. In 1889, although women were still unable to vote for a Member of Parliament, they were able to vote for the first time in the County Council elections.

In the new century, the Bathursts and the Masters did not have the monopoly on political power. Wealthy entrepreneurs such as the Cripps family, whose financial standing and influence on the economy of the town were further strengthened by marriage with other leading families of the day, also had political aspirations, and Joseph Cripps held his seat as an MP from 1818 until he resigned in 1841.

**MEMORIAL HOSPITAL c1950** C106034

The hospital was built in 1875 by the 6th Earl Bathurst, in memory of his first wife. The future use of the building has been the subject of much debate since the hospital moved to the larger, more modern, Querns.

# The Victorian Years of Industry and Expansion

**TOMB OF HUMFRY AND ELIZABETH BRIDGES IN THE PARISH CHURCH** C106074

One of the town's leading benefactors is depicted with his wife and children.

The 'Union' to which the politically unsure lady referred to was the workhouse under the Cirencester Union, which housed not only the town's poor and destitute, orphans, and those too debilitated to support themselves, but those from 38 other parishes as well. It came into being as a result of the Poor Law Amendment Act of 1834, and was built to house some 300 people on the site of the former parish 'Poor House' at Watermoor. The 1851 census records some 245 inmates, a figure that includes 100 children. Lord Bathurst had given a house in Chesterton for use as a workhouse as early as 1724, with the emphasis on 'work' for the poor to help defray the cost of their meagre meals and sparse accommodation on the parish. Joseph Cripps, whose business interests were vested in the family's banking, brewing and cloth manufacturing, gave a substantial sum in 1780 to help towards the maintenance costs of the workhouse. The building itself became the Cotswold District Council Offices in more recent years.

By the time the young Victoria's coronation was being celebrated in the streets of Cirencester - during which 'the poor' of the town made short work of some 536lbs of beef, followed by 2,200lbs of plum pudding, washed down by 564 gallons of beer, and made merry under the triumphal arches, listened to the band, and cheered themselves hoarse at the donkey races, all paid for by public subscription - the town's population had reached some 5,500.

Road transport was still by horsedrawn carriage and carrier's cart and the stage coach, against whose evils a writer in the 'Gleaner', a weekly paper published in Cirencester, warned in 1816:

'These stage coaches make gentlemen come up to London upon very small occasions which otherwise they would not do but upon urgent necessity; nay, the conveniency of the passage makes their wives often come, too, who rather than come such long journies on horseback, would stay at home. When they come up to town they must presently be in the mode, get fine clothes, go to plays and treats, and by these means get such a habit of idleness, and love to pleasure that they are uneasy ever after'.

Such pleasure-seeking would, however, have already been stirring in the bosoms of the town's matrons, to say nothing of the temptations that tantalised the impressionable young spinsters of that time, for Cirencester had many diversions to offer those with a 'love to pleasure'. Evening assemblies with music and dancing, teas, balls, recitals and recitations, performing infants, animals and human oddities of any disability or disfigurement, travellers bringing all manner of mimicry and quackery, and performers from fire-eaters to ballad singers entertained, amused and amazed the populace. Strolling players, companies of comedians and troupes of assorted thespians had performed in the town since at least the 1720s. The more superior companies brought their own booth theatres with them; others made do in what was described as a theatre in the yard of the 'Three Cocks', an inn that stood just off the Market Place in Castle Street. By 1816 the King's Head Hotel was hired for theatrical entertainments. But in 1794 Cirencester boasted its first purpose-built theatre, although its site has not been identified. It was described as 'small and warm and filled with genteel and numerous audiences every night' of its first season.

John Boles Watson, the driving force in theatre in the Cotswolds at the time, 'respectfully made known to the Nobility and Gentry of Cirencester' that his new theatre in Gloucester Street would be opened in 1799. According to Samuel Rudder, the town's historian and printer, the surrounding gentry did not patronise the town and its markets and activities but sought their pleasures in the fashionable spa towns of Cheltenham and Bath. However, there was more than enough patronage from the professional classes, who could fill the boxes at 3 shillings a seat, with brewers and mercers perhaps making do with the pit at 2 shillings, and the butcher, the baker, the tallow chandler, the cobbler and the boiler of soap, and any one of the workers who earned a meagre living at a dozen or so other trades of the town, treating themselves to a perch on the fixed benches that constituted the gallery for a shilling. A singular compliment to Cirencester and its principal noble family was Samuel Seward's Benefit performance as Harlequin, played against a specially painted backcloth depicting the Gothic folly at Oakley Wood. Whether his Lord Bathurst was among the patrons that night is not recorded, but certainly the rest of the audience would have been delighted to see such a familiar scene. The public had free access to the magnificent landscaped park - a privilege that the family has extended through the generations to this day. Among the list of notable actors of the age to tread the boards at Cirencester was the famous Sarah Siddons, who in 1807, as Mrs Beverley in 'The Gamester', had the audience 'repeatedly in floods of tears'.

## Did you know?

### From Theatre to Public House

*The theatre in Gloucester Street became the 'Loyal Volunteer' in the 1820s, one of the 70 or so recorded public houses in the town at that period.*

**GLOUCESTER STREET 1898** 42363

This unusual tile-fronted half-timbered building stood on the site now occupied by numbers 153 and 155.

# The Tontine Buildings

**THE TONTINE BUILDINGS 2004** C106709k *(June Lewis-Jones)*

These buildings were erected in Cecily Hill in 1802, at the time of the 3rd Earl Bathurst, who was Secretary of State for War and Colonies. As one of the original subscribers in the property, and obviously under the rules of 'tontine (a scheme based on a 17th-century French insurance policy) the last holder of this particular investment, the earl became the owner of the properties. Two of houses are now privately owned, the rest still belong to the Bathurst estate.

It would be interesting to know whether the visit in 1816 of the Duke of Wellington to the 3rd Earl Bathurst, had any bearing on the naming of the 'Loyal Volunteer' pub. The duke and earl were friends and there were a number of townsfolk in the cheering crowd who had been invited on to the Mansion house lawns to shake the hand of the hero of Waterloo. Or maybe it was a tribute to the loyal volunteers mustered in 1803 by the Earl Bathurst to supplement the militia on the resumption of hostilities against France. Training in the Park for the Cirencester cavalry force ended up as a bit of a jolly, after a mock battle was followed by the ladies being invited to picnic and dance to music

## The Victorian Years of Industry and Expansion

provided by the militia band. The realities and hardship experienced by the volunteers and their families when it came to fighting for real on foreign soil can only be guessed at by reading between the lines of the accounts of the Overseers of the Poor (serving men and assisting their families being the responsibility of the community). In 1856 the Royal North Gloucestershire Militia, first raised in 1757, had their headquarters and armoury in a purpose-built Barracks. They became the 4th Battalion of the Gloucestershire Regiment in 1881.

## The Barracks

**THE BARRACKS 1898** 40983

The castellated gothic-style building at the top of Cecily Hill and flanking the public entrance to the park is an outstanding architectural feature in this part of the town. After serving the military needs throughout the ages of war, the property was let to QA Training, who started to call it Cecily Hill Castle in the 1980s. It is now a forum for adult further education, under the auspices of Cirencester College. The name Castle continues in use, although most local people still refer to the building as the Barracks.

# The Bathurst Family and Estate

LORD APSLEY, heir to the famous Bathurst heritage, has a commitment to the understanding, care and conservation of the countryside and rural life in general, and to his home town in particular, that extends far beyond the traditional and expected 'noblesse oblige' of the old manorial lords. Reflecting on his position he says: 'I see myself as a townsman of Cirencester, and hopefully in a long line of short-term family custodians of the Bathurst Estate with the ambition of leaving it to the next generation in a sounder condition than when I entered it.'

**EXTRACT FROM VERSES BY EDWARD SMITH**
ZZZ00383 *courtesy of his son, Ralph Smith*

Edward Smith was the last oxman at Cirencester Park (see page 80)

**THE POPE'S SEAT 1898** 42360

The 1st Earl Bathurst, who inherited the Oakley Estate from his father in 1704, built this rusticated stone pavilion for his friend Alexander Pope, who was closely associated with the landscaping of the park and eulogised the earl and his estate in his poetry.

**PARK STREET c1960** C106111

# The Victorian Years of Industry and Expansion

**VIEW FROM THE OCTAGON 2004**
C106710k (June Lewis-Jones)

From the Octagon, another of the nine follies in the park, the view is southwards along the Windsor Ride.

The world's largest yew hedge, planted c1710, makes an impressive boundary to the Mansion House of the Bathurst estate.

**THE WOOD HOUSE 1898** 40975

Also known as Alfred's Hall, The Wood House is one of the many follies built to give interest to Cirencester's vast parklands. Generations of local people have enjoyed the privilege of using the area for various functions.

**LORD APSLEY (SEATED), ON THE OCCASION OF HIS 21ST BIRTHDAY** ZZZ00449 (Michael Charity)

*Left to right:* Lt Col Sir John Miller EVCO, DSO, MC; the Hon Alexander Bathurst (brother, now Major); Lady Henrietta Bathurst (sister, now Lady Henrietta Palmer); Countess Bathurst; and the 8th Earl Bathurst.

# CIRENCESTER – a history and celebration of the town

The origins of education in Cirencester are found way back in its past. A medieval Song School was conducted by a stipendary priest of the parish, and a public grammar school, first referred to in 1242, stood in Dyer Street. The next reference to the school records that in 1458 it was endowed with a chantry bequest by a Cirencester-born Bishop of Lincoln (perhaps an old boy of the school). This reference is generally accepted to be the origin of the latter-day Grammar School. Such was the pride of the townsfolk in their Grammar School that when the annuities which paid the schoolmaster's salary stopped as a result of the Dissolution, it was saved from closure by one of the town's charities. Following a successful period in Elizabethan times, the school declined under one Master Helme, due to his 'unscilfulness and slackness', but survived as an educational establishment and moved to Park Lane.

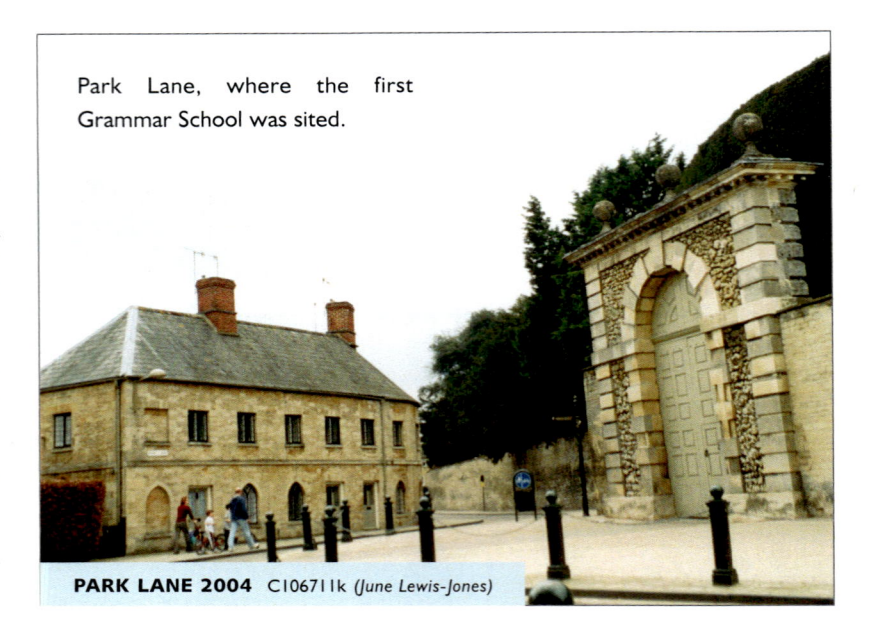

It appears that Grammar School masters during the 18th century were less influential than their pupils: it is recorded that in 1783 the master dismissed the school's one remaining pupil, returned to Oxford but still drew his salary! Fortunately for medical science, that was after Edward Jenner had been a pupil there and 'learned his letters with a little Latin and Greek', before going on to discover that injections of cowpox virus produced immunity against smallpox.

Park Lane, where the first Grammar School was sited.

**PARK LANE 2004** C106711k (June Lewis-Jones)

---

## Did you know?

### The Yew Hedge

*The yew hedge flanking the private entrance to the Mansion House is now approximately 12 metres (40 feet) high and takes 20 man-days to trim each year. The clippings are carefully saved and used in the treatment of various types of cancer.*

It is interesting that Peter Bathurst, the third son of Georgina, Countess Bathurst (sister of the 4th Duke of Richmond), was one of the first to be inoculated. The first anti-smallpox serum was taken by Dr Edward Jenner from a Gloucester cow called Blossom - and Lord Apsley, eldest son of the 8th Earl Bathurst, currently has a herd of some 60 of this ancient breed of Gloucester cattle on the Cirencester Park farm that he now runs as heir to the Bathurst estate.

In 1881 the Upper School of the Grammar School moved to new buildings in Victoria Road, joined in 1904 by the Cirencester Girls' High School that had been founded three years previously in premises in The Avenue. Among notable old pupils was the cricketing legend Walter Hammond, who while a boarder at the Grammar School so impressed his headmaster with his talent that he was recommended for County trials.

It is generally agreed that 'Wally' Hammond was the greatest figure in Gloucestershire cricket after the famous Dr W G Grace, and at his peak was reckoned as the world's finest batsman; only Don Bradman was considered to draw comparison with him. Little wonder, then, that the memory of the legendary 'Wally' Hammond being dismissed for a duck in an Old Boys of the Grammar School match in 1931 is treasured by all those who took part in it.

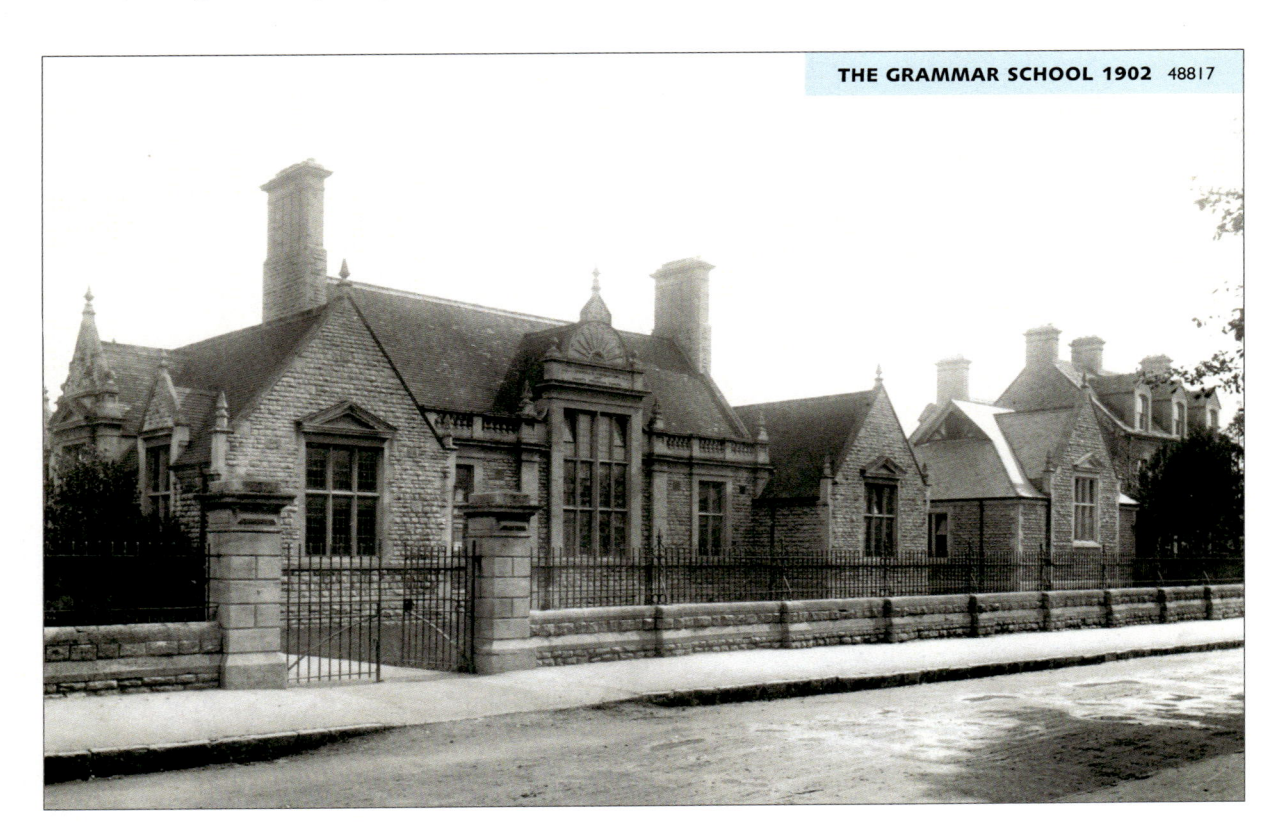

**THE GRAMMAR SCHOOL 1902** 48817

Grammar School Pupils and Staff September 1935 ZZZ00387 *(Ray Studios Ltd, Braintree; courtesy of Hilary Hainsworth)*

In a quite different field, the hundreds of children who were inspired and taught by Sir Peter Maxwell Davies during his time at Cirencester must have been delighted to hear of his appointment as Master of the Queen's Music. Cirencester led the way in comprehensive education in Gloucestershire: in 1966 the secondary schools at Deer Park were merged with the Grammar School, and by 1971 were in new buildings on the Deer Park site to the west of the town. Kingshill Comprehensive School followed five years later to the east, and the former Grammar School buildings in Victoria Road became a junior school.

Powell's School, still incorporating the tall Georgian building abutting the pavement in Gloucester Street, bears a plaque on the wall stating that 'Mrs Rebecca Powell by her will of 1722 was the charitable foundress of this school, erected and endowed 1740'. The Blue and Yellow charity schools merged under the name of Powell's School by an Order in Council at the Court of Windsor in 1876. Although on the same site, the schools were run separately, with houses attached for the respective Master and Mistress. Sometimes the proximity caused annoyance to one or the other, and there are references in the old records to 'the strange behaviour of females', which the master of the Boys School was obviously bemused by, as illustrated by one entry in the Log Book:

'1888, 23 April: The girls commenced their stamping gymnastics, the shaking of the floors and doors causing much alarm to Mr Young. Work suspended until the fit was over.'

This occurred again some years later:

'1892, 2 May: Violent outbreak of the stamping mania in the girls' room ... I sent for the Archdeacon to hear it, but found he was on a Visitation tour this week.'

As in other schools in the Victorian era, local distractions took the children away from their tedious lessons at every opportunity and greatly affected the attendance rate. The Log Book entries also give glimpses of

## The Victorian Years of Industry and Expansion

the hardship that touched so many of those young lives:

'1888, 14 May: Two boys, deserted by their father, taken to the workhouse.'

'1887, 26 Sept: This being "nutting week", Monday granted as the usual holiday. (Earl Bathurst opened his grounds to the public for collecting nuts).

Then, an observation on the changing social conditions of the time:

'1891, 14 Sept: A most remarkable reopening: no gleaning commences; no Fees. Only 109 present of 174 on the books. There are many parents whose means enable them to go to the seaside and elsewhere, and these show their position and contempt for gleaning by going off the last week in July or the first in August.'

Today's young Powellians still have as their school motto 'Steadfast in the Faith', and maintain strong links with the church, where a marble likeness of Rebecca Powell gazes impassively from her memorial in the Garstang Chapel.

**GLOUCESTER STREET 1898** 42363

**POST OFFICE 1898** 40970

Cirencester was served by a daily postal service on the mail coach run between London and Bristol from 1741.

The coming of the railway in 1841 to Cirencester (as the initial terminus of the Cheltenham and Great Western Union Railway from Swindon) generated both employment and more trading opportunities. Obviously very impressed with the speed at which business could now be transacted in person, the 'Gloucester Journal' reported that Mr Maurice Edwards, spirit merchant of Cirencester, travelled by means of the railway network to Birmingham and London 'and returned to Cirencester that same night, having travelled 268 miles within 23 hours'. Travel was already a world away from the time when Edmund Clutterbuck of London recorded in his diary a journey by stagecoach which he took in the summer of 1773. The ten-mile stretch from 'Cirencester to Hampton we ran in an hour, after dining at the Swan on peas and bacon and a neck of veal'. On the return journey, Mr Clutterbuck again stopped off at the Swan to change horses and 'made shift to eat very heartily on a boiled leg of lamb with greens and a couple of roasted chickens'.

The town's strategic position in the evolving road network was ideal for both passengers and goods, and within a week of Cirencester railway station opening, the 'Wilts and Gloucestershire Standard' reported that it had 'all the week exhibited the stir and bustle of a fair'. The distinctive station building was regarded by some as rather extravagant in view of its status as a terminus. The design is generally attributed to Brunel, but close scrutiny of railway station contracts points to it being 'supervised by his pupil Charles Richardson'. It was not until 1924 that it achieved its 'town' suffix. Another station was built at Watermoor, southeast of the town centre, and for many years there was competition between the two stations, particularly in the excursions they offered. In 1935 'Cheap Rail Trips from Cirencester Town' were advertised in the local paper, including 'half-day to Swindon and London, with a Sunday trip at the end of July to Cardiff and Barry Island'. The last passengers on the Cirencester Town railway travelled on 6 April 1964; the last to travel on the Cirencester Watermoor did so on 11 September 1961. The steeply gabled Cotswold stone building of Cirencester Town station still stands, making a distinguished punctuation mark in a chapter of the town's history and a handsome point for the coach and car park on the corner of Tetbury Road. Cirencester Watermoor station lingers on alone in the memories of an earlier generation: a roundabout siphons off today's traffic on the ring road, and the town's fire station and a modern housing development stand on the former goods yard and works site.

The canal age also touched Cirencester, for it was the terminus of a branch of the Thames and Severn Canal, which at just over a mile long connected with the main route at Siddington. No trace of that water artery remains in what was called the Cirencester Basin, between Querns Hill and Querns Road (previously known as Workhouse Lane). Warehouses at the wharf were converted into houses in the 1970s. The arrival of the first coal barges in 1789 attracted a great crowd to watch this new form of transporting heavy goods: salt, building materials and coal came in; mainly grain from the surrounding farms went out. The canal was eventually bought by the Great Western Railway in 1882, whose line at Watermoor had been its main competition, but trade dwindled, until coal was more or less the only cargo carried. Despite a major restoration programme, the canal trade petered out completely in Edwardian times.

Thanks to the dedication and commitment of a body of volunteer enthusiasts, great stretches of the Thames and Severn Canal have been restored over the last three decades.

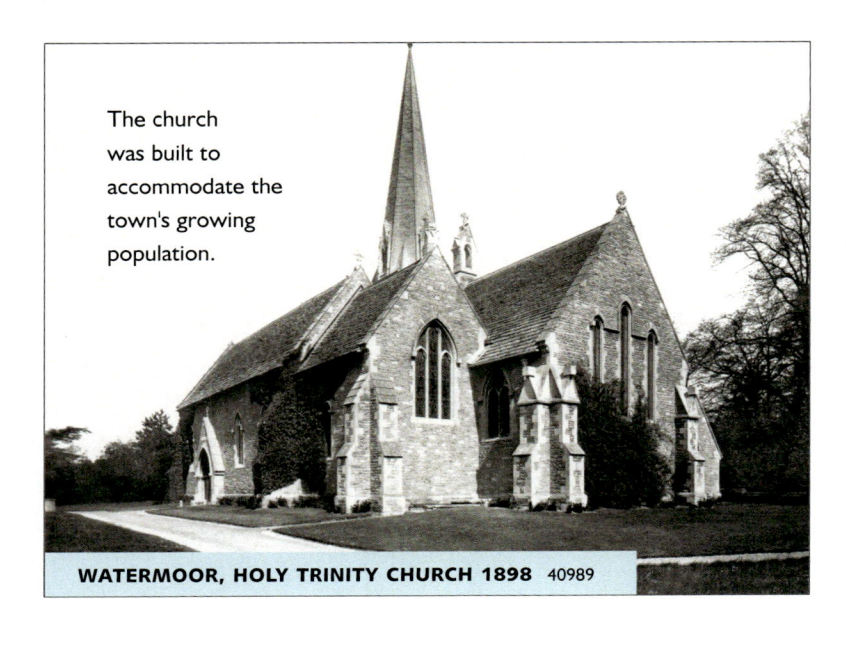

The church was built to accommodate the town's growing population.

**WATERMOOR, HOLY TRINITY CHURCH 1898** 40989

**THE CEMETERY AT HOLY TRINITY CHURCH 1898** 40992

An increased population in Victorian times meant siting a new cemetery away from the town centre.

Canal-side walks have been created so that everyone can enjoy the peaceful pleasure of walking in the steps of the tow men and their faithful companion horses.

Cirencester's role as a major market centre for the farmers of the fertile Cotswold countryside increased as methods of transporting heavy goods improved and better use was made of the purpose-designed cattle market that had been built by Earl Bathurst in 1867, on the Tetbury Road, in close proximity to the Cirencester Town railway station.

The Corn Hall had been built in 1863, when corn replaced wool as the staple commodity of the area. All passed now into rural folk lore are memories of the shepherd with a lock of wool on his smock, the carter with a band of whipcord twisted round his black felt billycock hat, and servant girls holding their mops, all standing around the Corn Hall, each bearing a token of their trade or calling, to advertise their availability for hiring. This open employment forum is as old as the Scriptures; locally the annual Hiring Fair was always called Cirencester Mop. Bands and booths provided music and all forms of entertainment, with inns doing a brisk trade in ale. The Corn Hall no longer serves its original purpose, but is today a trading and social centre.

The town lock-up, a small two-cell building with a distinctive domed roof, was moved

## The Victorian Years of Industry and Expansion

> ### Did you know?
>
> The last narrow boat to navigate the canal before it was finally closed to traffic was the 'Flower of Gloster', in 1911.

stone by stone in 1837 from the town centre to grounds in Trinity Road, to detain the recalcitrant inmates of the workhouse. It is now a listed heritage building under the care of the Corinium Museum service, which arranges a sequence of displays relating to the history of the county's lock-ups. Access is on request at the reception office of the Cotswold District Council offices in Trinity Road.

Makers of agricultural machinery and implements joined producers of edge-tools, carriages and cycles in the ever-increasing list of manufacturing industries centred on the town. In addition there was the gas works, milling and brewing. The Cole and Lewis bacon factory, foundries and the building trade extended the range of employment beyond the farms and grounds of the large estates, but as professional services and trades, particularly retailing, grew more successful, so too did the demand for domestic servants to support the households of the wealthier middle classes. A cursory glance at the 1881 census shows that well over 80 per cent of employed people were in domestic service of some sort, ranging from gardener's boys to grooms, and laundry maids to governesses.

**CASTLE STREET c1965** C106130

Little has changed in this street over the last 40 years.

# The Royal Agricultural College

The College was founded in 1845, with the aim of introducing scientific methods into agricultural practices and educating the country's future farmers, and was the first institution of its kind in the English-speaking world. Funds were raised by public subscription, with much of the support coming from wealthy landowners and farmers. The 4th Earl Bathurst, the College's first President, leased a farm of 160 hectares (400 acres) from his estate on which to build it. New buildings were designed in the Victorian Gothic style, but the ancient farmhouse and 16th-century tithe barn were retained. Ever since Queen Victoria granted the Royal Charter to the College in 1845, successive sovereigns have been patrons.

George Gibbs was a 23-year-old student at the College in 1892. According to his application form, he was an out student; he gave his local address as Ablington Manor, plus a London address at Queen's Gate Terrace. A testimonial of his moral character was undersigned by W C Gibbs, Clerk in Holy Orders at Hagley Rectory, and the certificate of application was signed by G H Gibbs (his father), and L B Gibbs (his mother) acted as guarantor. An additional point of interest about George's notebooks (leather bound and marked on the spine 'Agriculture' and 'Veterinary') is that spare pages at the back had been utilised by his brother, J Arthur Gibbs, for his own notes. From these he wrote the evergreen country classic 'A Cotswold Village', which has never been out of print since it was first published in 1898.

Of particular interest are his notes on hiring servants, where huntsmen are included in the same category as domestic servants, and his record of the many different sheep breeds in the College flock.

**EXTRACTS FROM THE LECTURE NOTES OF GEORGE HAROLD GIBBS 1892** ZZZ00377

ZZZ00378

# The Victorian Years of Industry and Expansion

**ROYAL AGRICULTURAL COLLEGE 1898**

CIRENCESTER – *a history and celebration of the town*

**CASTLE STREET 1898** 40971

This photo was taken soon after the major rebuilding of the northern side of Castle Street, commissioned by Earl Bathurst as part of the town centre improvements. J Arthur Gibbs, in his 'A Cotswold Village', commented '... we have never seen modern architecture of greater excellence than these Cirencester houses. They are as picturesque as houses containing shops possibly can be.'

The greatest topographical change to take place in the 19th century was the clearing of the tangle of ramshackle shops, inns and hovels, linked by mean and dark alleyways, in the town centre. Shoe Lane, Butter Row, Botcher Row, the Shambles and the old 'blind house' (a windowless lock-up) disappeared from the Market Place. So too did a number of houses that had been built up to the church porch, the wall of which had been weakened owing to the honeycomb of chimney flues built into it. All had gone by 1830 as a result of a Town Improvement Act, which Cirencester took to Parliament as a private Act, financed by the permitted sale of common land at Watermoor and Kingsmead. The spacious Market Place became the new forum, where the townsfolk gathered to watch the Vale of the White Horse Hunt Meet on Boxing Days, to enjoy the fun of Fair days, to shop at the market stalls, and to hear the proclamations as monarch succeeded monarch.

**CIRENCESTER ORDNANCE SURVEY MAP 1875 - 1882**

Tar Barrow
Tar Barrow
B.M. 420·1
B.M. 426·2
B.M. 412·2
B.M. 398·1
Grove Lane
City Wall
B.M. 363·0
B.M. 360·5
B.M. 365·5
Joe House
Sluices
B.M. 370·1
Ikenild Street
Foss Way
B.M. 371·7
Guide Post
Dyer Street T.P.
B.M. 363·7
R.C. Chapel
Old Quarry
The Beeches
B.M. 358·4
Corin Villa
Oxford Villa
Talbot Inn
Chester Ho.
Apsley Villa
The Nursery
Golden Lodge
B.M. 357·2
Royal Nursery
Almshouses
B.M. 359·6
Springfield Place
Somers Place
B.M. 358·0
Watermoor Ho.
Union Workhouse
B.M. 356·5
The Firs
Tesselated Pavement
B.M. 354·5
Trinity Church
(Chapel of Ease)
Grosvenor Cottages
Watermoor
Agnes Place
Victoria Place
Nursery
School
B.M. 368·0
Prospect Cottage
B.M. 356·7
B.M. 368·8
B.M. 354·5
Prospect Place
Corinium House
Denmark Cottages
Horse & Doll (P.H.)
B.M. 344·5
B.M. 343·6
Sluices
Ford
B.M. 397·9
B.M. 376·7
Pound Cottage
Pound
B.M. 365·7
Gas Works
Gasometers
Quarry
Nursery
River Churn
New Mills (Flock)
Sluice
Kingshill Quarry
Kings Hill
B.M. 379·1
Preston Forty
B.M. 353
CIRENCESTER

SEED MERCHANTS

VERDONE

CHAPTER FOUR

*1900-2000*
*A Century of Change*

THE NEW century was but a year old when the long Victorian era ended with the accession of Edward VII to the throne, but many of the changes that developed in the new age had already taken root in the 1800s. Women had started to have their voice heard in politics: suffrage was as important a topic as family welfare. The housewives of Cirencester channelled their support or opposition to their right to vote by affiliation to either the National Union of Women's Suffrage Societies or the National League for Opposing Women's Suffrage. There was active interest in the town according to the local paper of 1837, which reported that the working men's club (established in the 'Salutation Inn' in Cricklade Street) had drawn up a petition for universal suffrage which was 'being hawked about to every pothouse in the town and neighbourhood'.

Few of the agricultural labourers - who still made up the majority of the population - could afford 5d to buy the newspaper, which for the lowest paid amounted to a quarter of their weekly wage. And with the national Education Act still three and a half decades away, it is reasonable to assume that few would have been able to read it anyway. It was, therefore, the privately educated middle and upper classes that instigated the establishment of the public library and newsroom in Dyer Street as early as 1835, with the aim 'to excite a more general taste of useful reading and intellectual pursuits and to facilitate the progress of the studious'. Not everyone approved, however; there were some who feared the newsroom might be a focus of political excitement and unrest! The annual subscription fee of two guineas must have precluded any lowly folk from

**VIEW OF THE CHURCH FROM DYER STREET c1955** C106027

The cyclist is just passing Bingham House.

attempting to exercise their intellect, even though an Act of Parliament five years earlier had given boroughs power to establish public libraries - but made no provision for buying books until three years later!

Daniel Bingham founded the public library that still bears his name, now moved into larger more modern buildings behind Bingham House in Dyer Street, where it was first established in 1905. He also built Bingham Hall in 1908, as the venue for a whole host of activities, from lectures to dramatic performances. A row of villas in King Street also bearing the name of Bingham formed part of the endowment to finance these two great assets to the town. The legacy of these Cultural Assets (a phrase used by David and Linda Viner, Curatorial Advisers to the Trustees of the Bingham Library) is thought to be so important, that the centenary of their foundation is being celebrated over two years.

Without any doubt the most-thumbed of the newspapers and periodicals available in the old Reading Room would have been the 'Wilts and Gloucestershire Standard', which for 167 years has kept the people of Cirencester and district informed about news and events and provided a record for future generations. It was, and still is, as the editor, Peter Davison, says, 'first and foremost a provider of information. Along with the church, schools and numerous clubs and societies, the Standard remains a keystone of the community, helping to give everyone who lives and works in our town a sense of belonging, and despite competition from other newspapers, radio and television, and most recently the Internet, the Standard continues to be the town's first choice for news.'

It is generally acknowledged that it was the campaigning efforts of W Scotford Harmer, editor throughout the difficult years of the 1920s and '30s, that brought about the re-opening of the Royal Agricultural College after it had been closed for eight years during and after the 1914-18 war. The farm holding at that time was approximately 13 hectares (33 acres) and had been let to Mr Stewart, the Dairy and Poultry Manager, for the duration of the war. The College itself, together with the Principal's house, kitchen garden, outbuildings, grounds and cricket field, were let to Milton Court College, and

**LAND GIRLS** ZZZ00376 (W Dennis Moss)

Land Girls at the Royal Agricultural College Farm.

a number of students and staff joined the Forces. Among those who responded to the appeal to finance the re-opening of the College was perhaps its most illustrious ex-student, Viscount Bledisloe, who later became Governor General of New Zealand.

By the 1930s, under the Principal, Robert Boutflour, CBE, the student roll increased from 50 to 800. Boutflour initiated the vital College Diploma Course in Rural Estate Management and raised substantial funds to pay for new buildings. The outbreak of the Second World War found him urgently circulating students and their parents that the College was to be requisitioned for occupation by the Royal Air Force from September 1939.

The RAF arrived on the day after war was declared, and the College had to quickly rent out its farms, The Steadings and Fosse Hill, and dispose of all the machinery. It gave its Beagles Kennels to Cirencester Urban Council for use as the Cirencester Pig Club, and donated its beds and bedding to the evacuees who had arrived in the town. The Chapel and Bursar's house were exempt from the requisition order; it was decided that to safeguard the interests of the College while it was in government hands, the Bursar should remain on site in his residence! In 1943 the RAF rented the cricket field at £12 a year and requested the loan of the College's motorised lawn mower. The College re-opened in 1945, in the centenary year of its foundation, which was marked with a royal visit by King George VI and Queen Elizabeth the following year. In the last half of the 20th century the College expanded both

**ADVERTISEMENT FOR THE PICTURE HOUSE JULY 1935**
ZZZ00373 (courtesy of 'Wilts and Gloucestershire Standard')

**ADVERTISEMENT FOR STEELS GARAGE** ZZZ00379
(courtesy of 'Wilts and Gloucestershire Standard')

**ADVERTISEMENT FOR FAMOUS CICETER TAILORING BY SAMUEL CLAPPEN & SON**
ZZZ00374 (courtesy of 'Wilts and Gloucestershire Standard')

in size and curriculum, and in 1985 the first of many degree courses was started, in subjects ranging from rural skills and land management to communications technology and tourism. Up until 2001 it was completely independent of government funding and raised its income from tuition fees, conferences and functions, and from its farms, which now cover some 1,300 hectares (3,200 acres).

By the 1920s educational opportunities were becoming more equal, despite a tenacity to hold on to segregation of the sexes at the schools: former pupils can still recall today the high fence dividing the playgrounds at the Grammar School, where the boys and girls had separate entrances. Ralph Smith recalls his schooldays at Powell's School, where his father went, and where his own children and grandchildren have followed in the family tradition: 'We sat together, boys and girls in the same class for our lessons, but woe betide us boys if we got to the high wall and looked over at the girls at play, but we used to pass our little notes through the gaps in the stones to them.'

**GLOUCESTER STREET c1950** C106011

Edward Smith (Ralph's father) left Powell's School at the age of 12, having gained an exemption to work on Cirencester Park farm in the first year of the 1914-18 war. He had already proved his worth, having worked on Saturdays and school holidays for the previous three years, stone picking, thistle cutting and sweeping the walks for 7d a day to help out with the family housekeeping.

Despite the harsh working conditions and long hours, Edward had made up his mind that he did not want to follow his father's trade as a tailor. It was the land that called him. 'It appealed to me when working in the corn fields cutting thistles, with the corn tickling my knees and the larks whistling in the sky above, and I realised that farm work was to be my career, and I felt happy about it,' he recorded half a century later, in carefully formed handwriting on lined paper - just as he had learnt to do at school. In later years, on several occasions, Edward and his

**HAVE YOUR OWN ELECTRICITY**

Electric Light and Power are available anywhere at once at a running cost of less than 1d. per unit with a 'Diesel' Lister Plant. Installation can be made in a few days in an outbuilding; no skilled attention is required. Sizes available for all requirements from cottages to castles and industrial purposes. We shall be pleased to supply further information and to make recomdations without obligation.

**Williams & Ford**
127, Cricklade St. Cirencester

**ADVERTISEMENT FOR WILLIAMS & FORD**
ZZZ00375 *(courtesy of 'Wilts and Gloucestershire Standard')*

A 'Diesel' Lister Plant could provide electricity for 1d per unit.

**GLOUCESTER STREET IN FLOOD** ZZZ00372
*(courtesy of Ralph Smith)*

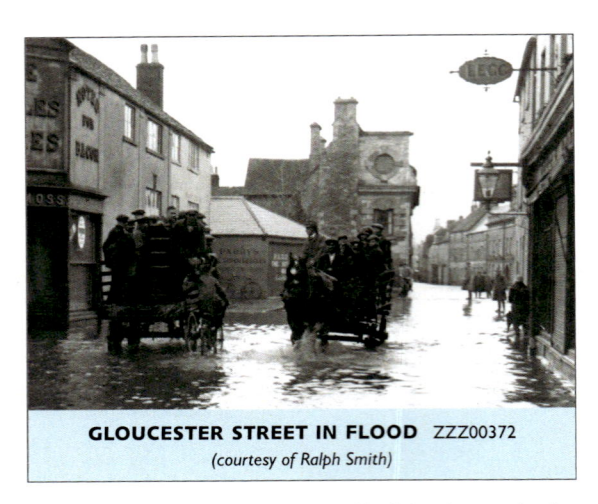

Gloucester Street in flood. Powell's School is at the far end on the left.

beloved oxen were called from the peaceful fields and woods of Cirencester to appear under the bright lights of the film studios - by then he had the last working team of oxen in the country. Recalling his early days, he wrote: 'When I started as an ox lad I had to be christened, this was done by the other ox men, who tipped a bottle of cattle medicine over my head - it was a black mixture prepared by the vet, Mr Blunsom. This was a very old custom and we ox lads all went through it whether we liked it or not.'

Ralph Smith and his sister Gwen were born in the Round House in Cirencester Park. 'The shepherd lived in the Square House,' Ralph recalls. He, like his father, worked all his life on the Bathurst estate, and between them they put in exactly a century of loyal service.

'We loved it when the Gloucester Regiment had their camp at the Barracks and we came down the Park to watch their Tattoo with all the soldiers smartly marching to their band. Old Sergeant Smith with his red sash on would be outside trying to get new recruits - his wife was a midwife and she biked up to our Round House to look after Mother when our Gwen was born.'

'It was only natural that I went on to the estate when I left school - it was our life, our home, no wonder that old poet, Alexander Pope wrote so romantically about it, and it was only just being created in his day - that was at the time of the first Earl Bathurst. My Dad wrote a poem, too, and I copied it out for him when I was at school - we had to practise our handwriting on poetry and I chose to do my Dad's in praise of Earl Bathurst's Park. I worked as a carpenter on the maintenance side, but I was always with

**WORKING OXEN AT PARK FARM** ZZZ00371
*(Fox Photos Ltd, London; courtesy of Ralph Smith)*

Edward Smith and his two-team ox-cart pass the carter, Wilf Gardner, who is driving the rubber-wheeled Fordson tractor that had replaced the horses. Reg Stevens is standing in the wagon.

my Dad with the oxen when I could be, and he would let me lead them when I was just a small boy when he got them all dressed up to draw a decorated wagon to parade through the town at Cirencester Carnival. My Dad thought it was a great honour and a wonderful tribute to the family's love of old country life when the old Earl Bathurst died and my Dad took him to the church from the Mansion House on the bier drawn by his favourite oxen.'

The bond between the Lord of the Manor and his workers is exemplified in the Smith family's high regard and deep respect for the Bathurst family. Such a bond was described in Richard Jefferies's book, 'Hodge and his Masters', written in 1879, where he commented on the 'pleasure of the annual social gatherings at the mansion, and it is apparent that something like a real bond exists between landlord and tenant. No false pride separates the one from the other - intercourse is easy, for a man of high and ancient lineage can speak freely to the humblest labourer without endangering his precedence.'

Jefferies compiled the book from a series of essays written when he was a young reporter on the 'Wilts and Gloucestershire Standard'. Fleeceborough in the book is our Cirencester. But it would appear that he was not a very good reporter - he missed meetings and failed to pick up the 'hot news' of the day, but his observations of the characters and characteristics of the rural market town, minutely detailed and written in poetic prose, earned him a place among the best of our country writers. There is an active Society devoted to his works in his Wiltshire birthplace of Coates.

The depressed state of agriculture of which Jefferies wrote continued until the First World War. As a consequence, in the local area there was a drift from the countryside into the town for work.

A plethora of Friendly Societies sprang up to assist members in financial and social difficulties. The concept behind these associations goes back to the distant past, reflecting what the first citizens of Cirencester, the Romans, did for their fellowmen.

**THE ROUND HOUSE** ZZZ00370 *(courtesy of Ralph Smith)*

Ralph Smith, on the far left, with his mother at the Round House in Cirencester Park, where he was born.

**CASTLE STREET c1965** C106104

R Scott & Co opened in Edwardian times as a working man's clothing shop - now it is a much-loved high-class 'County' gentlemen's outfitters. It is still very much a family business, and celebrates its centenary in 2004.

**DOLLAR STREET c1960** C106119

## The Cirencester Benefit Society

The Society, based in Castle Street, was founded in 1890, and had particular concern for the plight of the agricultural worker, who did not seem to be catered for in existing schemes. The Society's first meeting place was the 'Bell Inn' on the corner of the Market Place. The bell can still be seen in relief on the corner wall. (Advertisements for the business premises that took over the building carried the phrase 'At the Sign of the Bell'.)

The leading families of the day were the trustees of the Society, as recorded in the delightful old-style verbatim reporting, when even the ejaculations in response to the speakers' words were noted, as in the 1893 Annual Report, where Mr William Cripps pointed out the advantages of a Society in which they all knew each other: 'If the noble Chairman went, they had Oakley Woods and Cirencester House (laughter). If Colonel Master bolted, they knew where the Abbey was (laughter) - and they did say there was a little humble spot in the town called the Brewery in case their Treasurer went (loud laughter).'

---

Cirencester Brewery was one of the town's major manufacturers in the early 20th century. One of the posters of the First World War period combined a judicious piece of advertising within its patriotic call to help the war effort by stating: Order a Pint of Beer and drive a Nail into the Kaiser's Coffin. If you can't manage a pint, Order Half-a-pint and drive a Tintack. Drink the national beverage and help your country by paying your share of the War Tax.'

Guns were sited to protect the town's reservoir, and an air-raid hooter was set up on the Brewery in Cricklade Street; as it turned out it was so ineffective that the Council resorted to sending men on bicycles carrying placards to warn of any imminent air raids. Fortunately there was no significant enemy activity in the area, but the effects of action on the serving men were graphically illustrated by those who came from many different units and regiments to the Red Cross Hospital, set up in the Bingham Hall and Rifle Range in King Street.

Among the names of local men who did not return, recorded on the War Memorial by the parish church, is Lt William Niven, who joined the Berkshire Yeomanry and was killed at Gallipoli. He left a five-year-old son, David, who was later to become one of Hollywood's 'greatest Greats'. David lived with his mother at Golden Farm, until she remarried and moved from Cirencester.

**FIRST WORLD WAR ADVERTISEMENT TO HELP THE WAR EFFORT (AND LOCAL TRADE?)**
ZZZ00369 *(Wilts and Gloucester Shire Standard)*

- Fire, Ambulance, or Decontamination and Rescue. The report ended on the confident note that the 'valuable demonstration of the worth of the ARP services, which in the event of hostilities, will undoubtedly defeat the principal object of enemy air attack'. Hitler was obviously not impressed - war broke out six weeks later.

Cirencester publicised the arrangements for its Animal ARP: injured dogs and cats were to be taken to stables in Coxwell Street for examination before being transferred

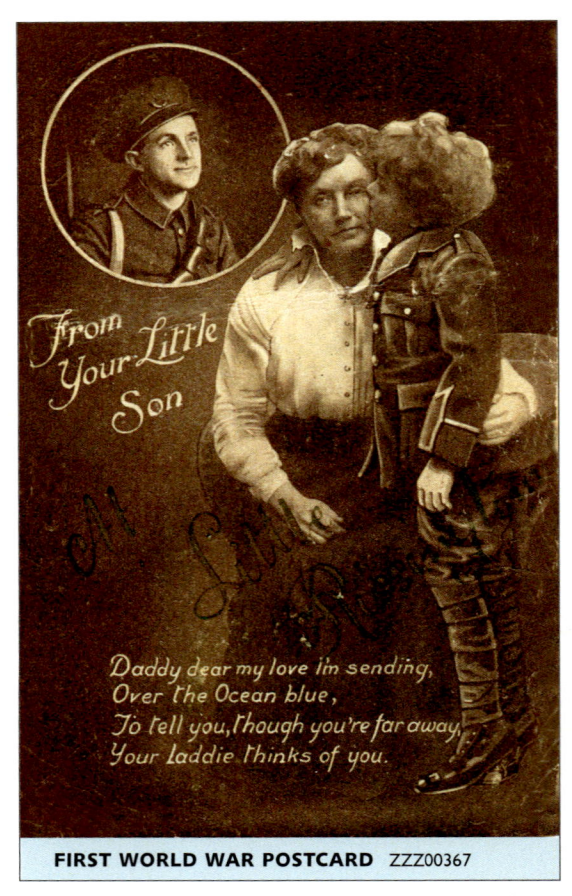

**FIRST WORLD WAR POSTCARD** ZZZ00367

'From Your Little Son'. Signed on the back: 'For daddie with love and kisses From Willie'.

As war clouds gathered over Europe for the second time, a mere two decades since the 'war to end all wars' ended, Cirencester prepared itself as a centre for ARP training, for the villages in the neighbourhood as well as for the town itself. Gloucestershire was the first county to have its ARP scheme described as 'exemplary'. In the 'Standard's report of a full-scale practice carried out in July of 1939, it remarked on the whole-hearted co-operation of everyone concerned and thanked the many people who had lent cars, which had sped from the town centre with a sign saying which emergency service they represented

*1900-2000 A Century of Change* 85

**THE MARKET PLACE c1960** C106060

The town War Memorial. The railings have now been removed, creating a peaceful spot where people can pause and reflect on the sacrifice of an earlier generation.

to the headquarters at number 11 Victoria Road. Major Duncan offered his premises in Lewis Lane as a shelter for horses, and advice was published on making a splinter-proof shelter for small pets by turning a dustbin on its side and heaping it over with soil. The town's wailing siren - the national signal of an impending air raid - had been a cause for concern since it was used in the First World War: Watermoor residents were still complaining that they could not hear it, and that Chesterton had whistles to blow in the street and they did not. The Council then approved a steam whistle on Cotswold Mills to augment the siren, and published a notice that tests would be carried out on the first Monday of each month. Cirencester Brewery claimed to be the first firm in the area to construct an air raid shelter (appropriately bearing a name plate, The Hop Leaf) for its staff, making it also available to the flat dwellers over their offices. Cellars were inspected by the ARP to check if they would make suitable shelters for people caught out in a raid while in the streets of the town. The shelter in the grounds of the old Memorial Hospital has been preserved and is the focus of exhibitions staged by the Living History Society - a valuable asset for school history groups. The old Museum of Roman

Antiquities - built by the 4th Earl Bathurst in 1856 to house his private collection, which he donated to the new Corinium Museum in 1938 - was used for storing sandbags until work began on filling them at the end of August 1939, and it was from here that gas masks were issued. Reports of accidents caused by the black-out filled the columns of the local press.

The test for the town's fire engine was to get two jets of water over the church tower - at 40 metres (132 feet), the tallest in the county. A massive water tank was situated opposite the church - covered with wire netting after the lively New Zealanders stationed in the town

**SCHOOL PARTY** ZZZ00365 (June Lewis-Jones)

Schoolchildren visit the air raid shelter that has been preserved for war memorabilia displays.

**SCHOOL PARTY** ZZZ00366 (June Lewis-Jones)

A school party is led by Peter Grace, founder member of the Living Memory Historical Association, to see the air raid shelter in the Memorial Hospital grounds. The imposing building in the background, redesigned from an earlier non-conformist chapel, was the annexe and X-ray department built as a memorial to the town's 209 servicemen lost in the 1914-18 war.

took to dunking each other in it following a night out at the local hostelries - and a smaller tank opposite the Corn Hall. The weathercock on top of the tower suffered a hole in the tail one night after one of the crack shots fulfilled a bet. Brian Carter was one of the impressionable young lads to be overawed at the time, both by the temerity and accuracy of the action, and says that the commanding officer had verified that the shot was from a Lee Enfield. Church weathercocks were obviously a popular target, as Derrick Youngs was to discover when he found the one at Fairford had also got a bullet hole in the tail. When Derrick repaired the one at St Mary's he found the maker's name sandwiched between the two body halves: Joseph Packer, Maker, Cirencester 1843. 'It is identical to the one on top of Cirencester parish church,' says Derrick, 'They must have hatched from the same clutch of church cock eggs!'

'A sorry procession, but surprisingly brave' was how the 'Standard' described the first contingent of evacuees to arrive at Cirencester on Friday 1 September 1939. Many clutched teddy bears and dolls in their hands and looked tired, with swollen eyes telling of tears shed at parting from their parents. Some 474 children with 58 teachers and helpers arrived, far fewer than the 800 anticipated in June when the railway personnel had been kitted out with red armlets to deal with the urban area and white for the rural district.

Local schools bulged at the seams with the influx of evacuees. Iris Norman recalls returning to the Grammar School a few days after she had 'left school' to become a Pupil Teacher at Miss Goodworth's Kindergarten for £10 a term. Instead of peeping through the dividing wall of the playground to watch schoolboys, she could now watch soldiers at drill. Units of the armed forces swelled the population of the town, public buildings were requisitioned and many premises lost their iron railings for scrap metal. Fund-raising events to help the war effort ranged from moonlight skating on the frozen lake in Cirencester Park to ambitious plans by the Urban District Council: 'Shall Ciceter present the Royal Air Force with a Spitfire - the cost of one of these nippy little fighters which have struck terror in the hearts of the Nazis is generally put at £5,000, can Cirencester find it?' It was decided that 'the District' should be invited to contribute, but the county National Farmers' Union declined as they thought they

## The Black-Out

One commercial traveller declared Cirencester to have the blackest black-out in the country. Through the Letters to the Editor page of the 'Standard' he announced that he would be giving the town a miss until the war was over.

'Spotter' of the 'Standard' reported that he had fallen over the Army and the RAF - at least one representative from each of those Forces - as they lay on the pavement in 'darkest Cirencester' after colliding. A 'volley of well-modulated abuse at the black-out' followed, then 'Spotter' helped them to the nearest hostelry, 'where butter was applied to the bumps and beer to the stomachs'.

**STAFF AT CIRENCESTER HOSPITAL** ZZZ00368 (W Dennis Moss)

Staff in charge of Air Raid organisation at the Hospital between 1939 and 1945.

were 'big enough to raise a fund themselves, not for a Spitfire - but a bomber!' Despite a huge campaign and much individual effort the town failed to buy a nippy little Spitfire - but 'Cirencester' was proudly emblazoned on the side of a Sherman tank as part of the Tanks for Attack scheme.

As women were called on more and more to fill the place of men who had joined the armed forces, war nurseries were started to look after pre-school-age children: Cirencester had its first in the Querns House and later in a single-storey building in Abbey Way. The school dinner scheme was started, a British Restaurant opened in the Church Hall in Cricklade Street, and Joan Haddrell and her group of Girl Guides were given the task of training the WI and the WVS to cook on an open camp fire and use the old rural haybox for slow cooking.

Cirencester WVS earned special praise for its 600 members, who did everything from scrubbing floors to cooking meals at the 'feeding centres'. In addition they performed voluntary night duties at the Memorial Hospital, where casualties from the Front were first brought in, and kept confidential reports on each evacuee child to monitor his or her well-being. Evacuees were treated for minor ailments and injuries in a room over John Smith's the corn merchants in Cricklade Street. 'Making the most of it despite stringent rationing' seemed to be the unwritten slogan of morale-boosting local news and propaganda, which at the first Christmas of the war declared: 'A right happy time' was had by all, with some 223 roast beef dinners enjoyed over two days at the British Restaurant, thanks to the organisation of Mrs Sackley. It ended with the cheering thought that 'porridge would be cheaper in the New Year'.

As the war years dragged on and rationing became more acute, paring close to the bone, literally, was the skilled job of Fred Haddrell at Jesse Smith's - the main slaughterhouse in the town. Cattle trucks were requisitioned by the Ministry to transport meat to the old livery stables in Dyer Street, from where it was rationed out to the local butchers. Cattle were often walked down to the slaughterhouse, led by a pair of oxen. One dinner-time two men delivering a consignment of tinned corned beef to the old cottage at the back of Jesse Smith's butcher's shop for safe keeping were trapped inside for over an hour by Fred's dog, who had been taught 'to guard the rations'. Many medical supplies were reliant on the slaughterman's skill. A whole list of products - from indigestion tablets to face powder, hair cream and surgical gut for stitching wounds - was made from the buckets and barrels of glands, spinal columns and general gall so expertly extracted and saved from the work 'at the back'.

**CRICKLADE STREET c1965**  C106118

**MARKET PLACE c1955** C106047

Charles Barnett's fish, meat and game shop on the corner was open-fronted in the old style for years. It is now closed, but Jesse Smith's award-winning family butcher's shop is just round the next corner, in Black Jack Street.

Every available bit of land went under the plough or the humble spade in the Dig for Victory campaign. School gardens and allotments appeared everywhere, but the countryman's passion for his national game saved the town's cricket grounds. Walter Hammond, together with Charles Barnett, another local lad of national cricketing fame, exchanged their white flannels, boots and cable pullovers for the uniform of the armed forces. Herr Hitler was warned, however, through the pages of the local press, that these were formidable chaps with a bat so he had better look out when they changed it for a gun! In 1941 Cirencester Cricket Club held a meeting at Viners baker's shop to determine how best they could carry on when there were only two other teams known to be still playing - Cheltenham and Swindon GWR. The question of the outfield was raised, but Mr Berkeley Stephens who chaired the meeting said that it would take the game back to what it was 50 years ago, so they 'would just have to hit a bit harder'.

> **Did you know?**
>
> *An Emergency Committee was set up to safeguard the interests of Gloucestershire County Cricket during the Second World War.*

Passion was once again aroused in parochial breasts in October 1940, when it was seen that the war had left the town without a band to head its parade of the Home Guard, which was 'impressive in size and bearing'. The village band of Chedworth was called upon to fill the gap. It was reported that: 'At one time the appearance in Cirencester of a band from Chedworth was an occasion to arouse political feeling to a high pitch'.

Warnings were issued to everyone from everywhere on every conceivable subject. The War Agricultural Executive Committee warned farmers that they could be displaced from their farms if they did not meet the 'efficiency' standards, and the farmers warned the said Committee that if their wives got to know of 'your Committee suggesting that they should undertake the duties of fire watching when they are working as hard as the men, coping with evacuees in their home and doing more than their bit for the war effort, you may have to close and barricade your doors'. Local people were able to watch one aerial dog fight over the town one Sunday afternoon, as Mrs Muriel Gough recalls:

'The family was at a Salvation Army open air meeting when a German bomber flew over and was shot down by one of our planes. My father, who came out of retirement to take the place of the news reporter who had joined the Army, immediately got out his bike and cycled out to Coates to the scene of the crash. He was most indignant that so many people followed on their bikes 'sight seeing'. It was gruesome, but his report for the paper couldn't say as much. I remember walking through the blacked-out streets that night to post his report to catch the 11pm town postal service.'

Parish magazines as well as newspapers had to conform to censor regulations, so reports of raids and air crashes, even local weather reports (useful to the enemy, particularly in view of the plethora of airfields in the Cotswolds), gave little or no detail.

**SQUARE DANCING** ZZZ00362

Square dancing was introduced to the Cotswolds by American Forces.

Among the many outsiders who came to know Cirencester during the war years were units from the Allied Forces at the American Hospital built in Deer Park. Glenn Miller and the USAAF Band visited the patients there in August 1944. Other temporary residents included New Zealand foresters felling timber on the estate, German and Italian prisoners-of-war working on the farms, Polish free fighters, and evacuated city children. An Americans-only clubroom at the Bingham Hall was named Doughnut Dugout by the locals, and a jitterbug craze hit the town after it held its first Jitterbug Contest, organised by the evacuated staff of the Texas Oil Company. Sounds of everything from 'Truckin' to Boogie Woogie to Alec Mattock's augmented band reverberated throughout the old Corn Hall, and the Memorial Hospital was £43 10s better off because of it.

## Cirencester's Secret Agent

Cirencester can claim to have had at least one secret agent: Kenley Lass - or Pigeon NURP 36JH190, to give the brave little bird her full military title. Bred by Donald Cole of the 'Bull Inn' in Dyer Street, she was the first pigeon in the Second World War to be awarded the Dickin Medal, the animals' VC. The citation reveals that she was 'used with success for secret communications from an Agent in enemy-occupied France while serving with the NPS (National Pigeon Service) in October 1940'. Kenley Lass was parachuted behind enemy lines with a British Agent and remained hidden with him for eleven days before being released to fly back to base with her message - a flight of some 300 miles, which she achieved in one day. She carried out a similar mission in February 1941.

**CIRENCESTER PIGEON " V.C."**
BROUGHT FIRST NEWS FROM OCCUPIED FRANCE
Kenley Lass, owned by Mr. Donald Cole, Bull Hotel, Cirencester was presented with the Dickin Medal (" Pigeon's V.C.") for meritorious performances on War service.

**KENLEY LASS AND HER DICKIN MEDAL** ZZZ00364
('Wilts and Gloucestershire Standard')

**EDWARD SMITH, ENGLAND'S LAST OX-MAN** ZZZ00363 *(W Dennis Moss; courtesy of Ralph Smith)*

Edward Smith in the Deer Park, just before the American war-time hospital was built. Deer Park School and Cirencester College are now on the site.

The Market Place became the forum for the Victory celebrations, with bonfires, bunting, singing and dancing. Street parties, with ancient trestle tables groaning under piles of goodies, were enjoyed by all after the restrictions and anxieties of the war years. The long list of local names on the Roll of Honour that joined those from the First World War gives a glimpse of the human cost.

Cirencester was unscathed by any direct enemy action, and immediate post-war building was for housing its increased population. New schools, hospital and medical facilities, shops and car parks, leisure facilities

**MARKET PLACE 1898** 40965

# CIRENCESTER – *a history and celebration of the town*

**THE POLICE STATION c1965** C106128

The Forum car park is on the right, its name perpetuating the Roman Forum – the meeting place of the ancient city.

and community centres, light industry and new roads followed.

As a result of local government re-organisation in 1974, the former Urban District Council ceased to exist, replaced by the Cotswold District Council and Cirencester Town Council. This meant that for the first time in its long history, Cirencester could have a mayor. The Arms of Cirencester incorporate symbolic elements of the town's history: from the Roman capital and battlemented wall above which the legendary Phoenix rises (the town symbol since the 17th century), to an arm holding a scythe, with green and gold colouring to represent the richness and importance of the agricultural area of which it has always been the centre.

**VISIT OF DIANA, PRINCESS OF WALES 1982**
ZZZ00361 *(Michael Charity)*

The princess at Lewis Lane Playgroup.

**CARNIVAL FLOAT** ZZZ00360

The drive to get Britain back to normal is reflected in this post-war carnival entry. Mycalex was one of the biggest local employers at the time.

## Eric Cole, Local Architect

A vast amount of the architecture in Cirencester and district of the post-war period is the work of the late Eric Cole, whose local firm still sets the benchmark for traditional Cotswold style. Along with a number of private houses and conversions of buildings, his work includes a diverse range of period designs: the Roman style doorway to the Corinium Museum, the 'new in the Fifties' local Territorial Army Centre, Bailey Lodge, the Principal's House and Boutflour Assembly Hall at the Royal Agricultural College, and the Jubilee Lamp 'erected by the Inhabitants of Cirencester to commemorate the Silver Jubilee of His Majesty King George V 1900-1935' that stands in Dyer Street close to the entrance to the Forum.

**ERIC COLE IS CONGRATULATED BY HER MAJESTY QUEEN ELIZABETH II 1953** ZZZ00350
*(Cheltenham Newspaper Co Ltd; courtesy of Mollie Coton)*

# Eric Cole, Local Architect

To meet an exacting challenge for a reasonably priced bungalow that could be enlarged and adapted to suit each individual family, Eric Cole chose cedarwood instead of indigenous Cotswold stone. His design, which brought congratulations from the Queen when it was exhibited at Earls Court in 1953, was shown on television and eventually formed part of the New Mills development. After his appointment as architect to the Urban District Council, Lt Col Cole was responsible for designing housing estates at Chesterton, Abbey Way, Bowling Green, Beeches, London Road, The Mead and New Mills.

**JUBILEE LAMP 2004**
C106712k *(June Lewis-Jones)*

**THE BEECHES ESTATE c1955** C106026

1900-2000 A Century of Change

A reproduction of Mr. Eric Cole's drawing of the Cirencester Urban District Council's new chambers and offices. The original was presented to the Council by Mr. Cole on the occasion of the official opening of the premises.

**DRAWING FOR CIRENCESTER URBAN DISTRICT COUNCIL'S CHAMBERS AND OFFICES** ZZZ00351

HOPE'S STANDARD METAL WINDOWS for STONE BUILT HOUSES

A COTTAGE ON THE ABBEY ESTATE, CIRENCESTER.  Eric Cole, Architect
Holborow & Sons, Builders
The total cost of this house, including land, was £910 . 0 . 0. The metal windows with leaded lights and wood frames complete cost £30 . 0 . 0

**A COTTAGE ON THE ABBEY ESTATE** ZZZ00352

## Local firm's new houses impressed Queen Mother

THE Cirencester Urban District Council have a strong claim to be pioneers of the idea behind the Government's new scheme to bring house-ownership within the reach of the family man of small means.

Under the scheme, announced on Monday by Mr. Harold Macmillan, the Minister of Housing and Local Government, a person will be able to purchase a £2,000 house by putting down as little as £100.

Some time ago the Cirencester U.D.C. began a scheme whereby they would finance people wishing to erect a type of factory - made cedarwood permanent house on the New Mill Development Site.

They were willing to advance up to 90 per cent of the total cost of erecting this type of house on the estate, the capital to be paid back over a period of up to 30 years, at around £2 a week, plus 10s. for rates.

### IMPRESSED BY PROJECT

Building societies would generally advance only 75 to 80 per cent of their valuation of the house, leaving the buyer to find cash for the rest.

The approved houses were to be made by Neata Products (Cheltenham) Ltd., specialists in agricultural buildings, village halls, and pavilions.

This firm, with their consultant architects (Eric Cole and Partners, of Cirencester) had worked out plans for combining the cost advantages of factory unit - building with many of the advantages of practices adopted in building traditional types of homes.

The Cirencester U.D.C. were impressed by the project, especially as their request to the Government for special permission to build houses for sale under the Acquisition of Small Dwellings Act, 1947, included the Neata type house.

At present the Cheltenham firm has one of its two-bedroom cedarwood homes erected at the Earls Court section of the British Industries Fair, in London.

### ROYAL APPROVAL

On Tuesday it was inspected by Queen Elizabeth, the Queen Mother, and Princess Margaret.

Mr. Bernard Glassman, Managing Director of the firm, told the "Echo": "The Royal visitors were tremendously enthusiastic about the home.

"The Queen Mother told me that she was extremely happy that this type of dwelling was being made available to the public, and that it was being erected in various parts of the country.

"She told me she thought our home was 'so gay, so bright and so colourful.' There was no doubt that she and the Princess were absolutely charmed by it. They stayed a long time, having a most thorough look at it."

The Queen Mother was told that the house she was viewing cost £711 on leaving the Cheltenham works, and could be erected fully ready for occupation at a total cost of £1,700.

### THE TURNING POINT

Before Mr. Macmillan announced his new scheme, the Cheltenham and Gloucester Building Society was willing to advance a loan of up to 72 per cent of the cost of the cedarwood house, to be paid back over a period of 15 years. In doing this, it recognised the dwelling as being virtually as good a "risk" as an ordinary brick-built house.

Neata Products first showed their new type of house at the 1947 British Industries Fair. "We knew that there was no hope of selling them then because of the Government restrictions," said Mr. Glassman. "But we were confident that the day would come when things would be quite different.

"The great turning point in our fortunes was when we got the Cirencester R.D.C. interested in them sufficiently to give us their backing.

"The effect of the new Government announcement is likely to be simply terrific. In fact, the scheme might well have been 'tailor-made' for us.

"At present, we are employing around 150 people at our Leckhampton works. But we have planned all along for a rapid expansion if it became necessary, as it now looks as though it might."

The firm is now in the process of drawing up a nation-wide list of approved builders whom customers can approach to erect the homes when they are delivered.

Prices of the components of the two and three-bedroom houses range from £650 to £711. Building costs, converting the components into a home ready to occupy and connected to all services, etc., add another £888 to £987.

The manufacturers claim that they are offering "by far the finest value in housing obtainable today."

One of the orders just obtained at the B.I.F. is for 14 of the homes, placed by a Swiss concern.

Says Mr. Glassman: "We consider it quite an achievement to get an order from Switzerland, the home of the wooden chalet. The purchaser told us that they had nothing to compare with our building out there."

An important feature of the Cheltenham-made homes is their very up-to-date interior and general design.

**NEWSPAPER CUTTING** ZZZ00353

THE NEW Bailey Lodge. Right: Mr. S. W. Fordham receiving the key to the door from Mr. Eric Cole.

## Gift house for principal is opened

"A substantial donation" from a charitable trust established from part of the estate of a Matlock, Derbyshire, agricultural merchant, has paid for a new house for Mr. F. Garner, principal of the Royal Agricultural College, Cirencester.

Yesterday, when the house, Bailey Lodge, was opened by Mr. G. W. Fordham, governing director of Messrs. E. H. Bailey Limited, of Matlock Mills, it was also disclosed that money provided by the trust had financed alterations within the college enabling a further member of the staff, and his wife, a nursing sister, to live there.

In addition some 15 to 20 extra students can now be accommodated within the main college building.

Mr. Fordham is one of the trustees of the Ernest Bailey Charitable Trust and he was accompanied by the other trustees, his wife, and Mr. B. C. Orme.

He explained that as the trust received part of its income through agriculture, it had been decided some funds should be returned to foster agricultural interests.

**NEWSPAPER CUTTING** ZZZ00354

## New bungalow to be televised

Television films are to be made on Saturday of a two-bedroom bungalow erected at the British Industries Fair at Earls Court which has been designed by the Cirencester architects, Eric Cole and Partners, and built by Messrs. Neata Products of Cheltenham.

It is expected that the Queen will inspect the bungalow when she visits the Fair.

Built of red cedar-wood, which in Great Britain and other countries has been used in the construction of centuries-old buildings, the bungalow can be enlarged in the same way as a well-known type of bookcase can be expanded by the addition of extra units. Cost is variable according to the means and wishes of its purchaser.

**NEWSPAPER CUTTING 1953** ZZZ00355

# 1900-2000 A Century of Change

## Neata CEDARWOOD HOMES

One of a range of our attractive CEDARWOOD HOMES now being erected on THE NEW MILL DEVELOPMENT SITE at CIRENCESTER. These are immediately available for the home market, and prices range from £1,400 complete, on your site.

Loans through the Small Dwellings Acquisition Act or mortgages can be arranged.

### SEE ONE AT THE B.I.F.

One of these houses, completely furnished by "Modern Woman," is being exhibited on our STAND No. R.14, EARLS COURT, MAY 3rd to 14th.

**ADVERT FOR CEDARWOOD HOMES**
**1953** ZZZ00356

**MR ERIC COLE** ZZZ00358

## Ciceter Spotlight

### A BUSY MAN

One of the most elusive men of my acquaintance in these "dog days" in Lieut.-Colonel Eric Cole. In ten days I have failed to make contact with him, whether my call has been made in person or by telephone. There can be few men of so many interests, or who are called so many ways at once.

At the moment, I gather, he is settling into his new office of President of the Gloucestershire Architects Association, into which he was installed on July 1st.

Directly connected with the Royal Institute of British Architects, this Association includes in its membership practically all the practising architects of the county. Colonel Cole has earned his position as its president by active membership of its committee for many years, officiating as chairman of its Public Relations Committee, and, for the past two years, occupying the post of vice-president—a full apprenticeship for his present position.

One of the first duties with which the Association will be concerned under his presidency will be of somewhat unusual nature. The Association has been asked by the Corporation of Cheltenham to take part in the British Festival of Art at Cheltenham, and to undertake the restoration of the important Regency building, the Pumproom at Pitville.

This is probably the first occasion in this county that an association has undertaken a civic task of this kind.

• • • •

### Great Variety

In Cirencester one can hardly turn around without being confronted with work which he—or his firm Eric Cole and Partners—has carried out. The Corinium Museum, the Jubilee Lamp, the Chesterton Estate, "Easiform" houses modified to blend with houses of traditional type, Cotswold type houses on Abbey Way, Bowling Green estate, and the still growing Beeches and London Road estate. So, at some time or other, he must put in quite a considerable amount of time in his office . . .

"Give me two-six-eight again, please."

". . . not in the office . . ."

"I was afraid of that answer. Will you ask him to ring . . . . Oh, what's the use!"

He won't have gone to South Africa, or the South of France, though he has done work in both places. Nor is he likely to have gone to India, where, among other work, he built an airport during his military service.

An S-O-S! Should this meet his eye during the week-end, perhaps Colonel Cole would be so good . . .! This is a genuine call.

**NEWSPAPER CUTTING**
ZZZ00359

---

JRDAY, APRIL 25, 1953.

### DESIGNED BY LOCAL FIRM

**Bungalow will be Inspected by the Queen**

A Cirencester firm of architects has been responsible for designing a bungalow which the Queen proposes to inspect during her visit to the British Industries Fair at Earl's Court on Monday.

The architects are Messrs. Eric Cole and Partners, who were recently appointed consulting architects to Neata Products Ltd., of Leckhampton, Cheltenham. The firm asked Messrs. Cole to produce some designs for bungalows, the conditions being that the houses should be small but adequate, and capable of being adapted or enlarged in small units to suit the individual taste and pocket.

It is one of the designs submitted that has now been erected at Earl's Court, one of four buildings exhibited by Neata Products. The bungalow is a cedarwood structure, following a tradition of timber houses which have existed in many parts of the world for centuries.

There are in the vicinity of Cirencester a number of cedarwood houses erected before the war, and about 200 years ago there were quite a number in England, notably in Kent and Essex. At that time in the Cotswolds, the area's natural building material, stone, was more readily to hand, but since the development of the internal combustion engine it has been economically possible to transport materials from different parts of the country, and indeed of the world.

Red cedarwood has the advantage, if left untreated, of toning down with the greys of the Cotswolds.

### PARTLY PREFABRICATED

This particular series of bungalows is partially prefabricated, and therefore easy for transport. By building in sections, they can be adapted to suit the type of plan required. Another advantage, of course, is that the houses can be quickly erected, yet after assembly they will be rigid and durable.

When the prototype was first erected at the British Industries Fair, it was found to be too close to one of the stancheons of the building, and authority was given for an extra six feet of space to be given to the exhibitors. The whole building was simply hauled the six feet away from the stancheon without any effect on the structure!

Internally, the fittings and furnishings are left to the taste of the individual client or builder, but the walls are in cedar and the roof is shingled. The only brick or stone used in the bungalow is in the main fireplace.

The total cost of erection for a bungalow comprising living room, two bedrooms, kitchen, outbuildings, W.C., bathroom, linen cupboards and wardrobes works out at about £1,500, complete with drainage, fittings and a certain amount of fencing.

**NEWSPAPER CUTTING 1953**
ZZZ00357

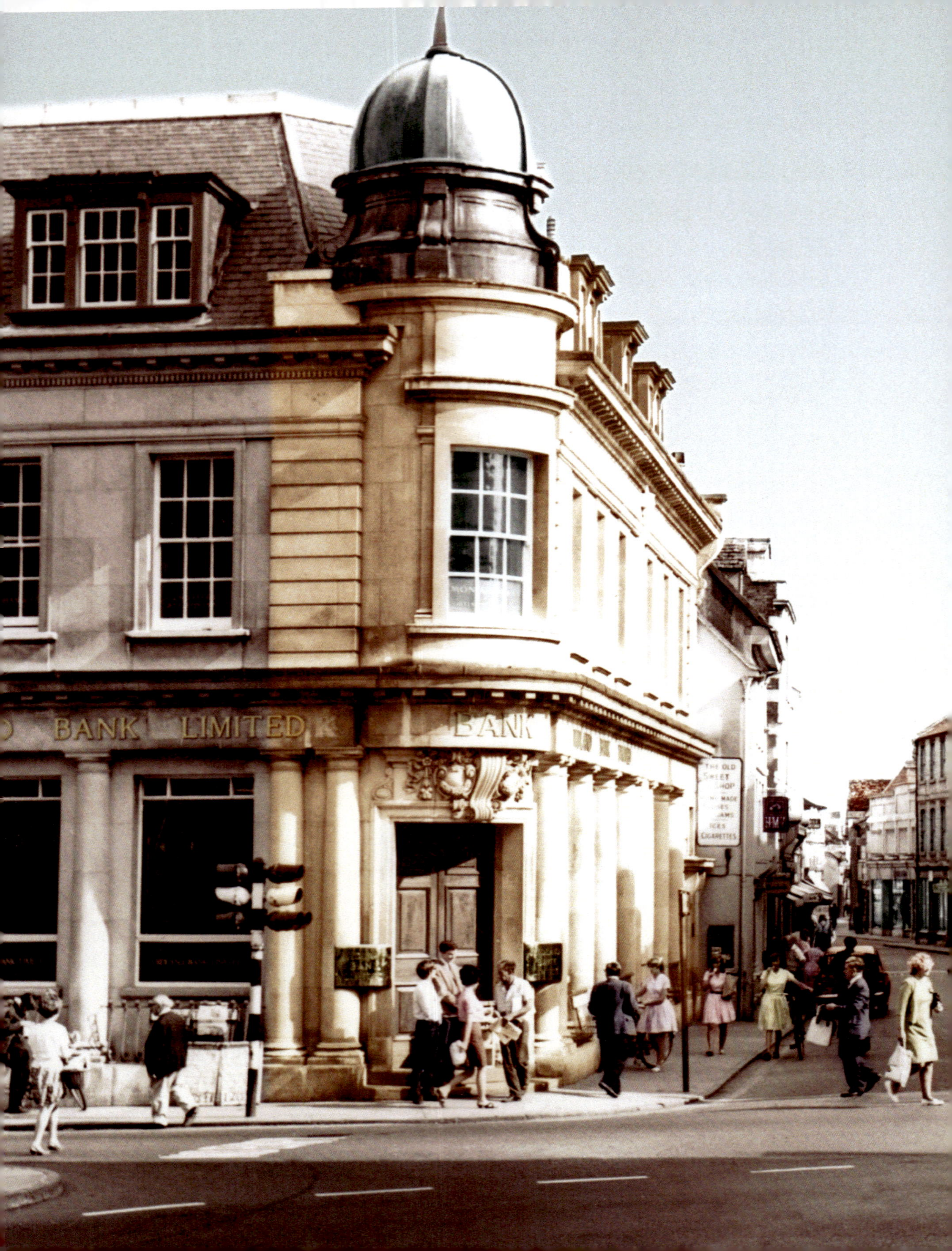
BANK LIMITED
BANK
THE OLD
CIGARETTES

**CRICKLADE STREET c1955** C106113t

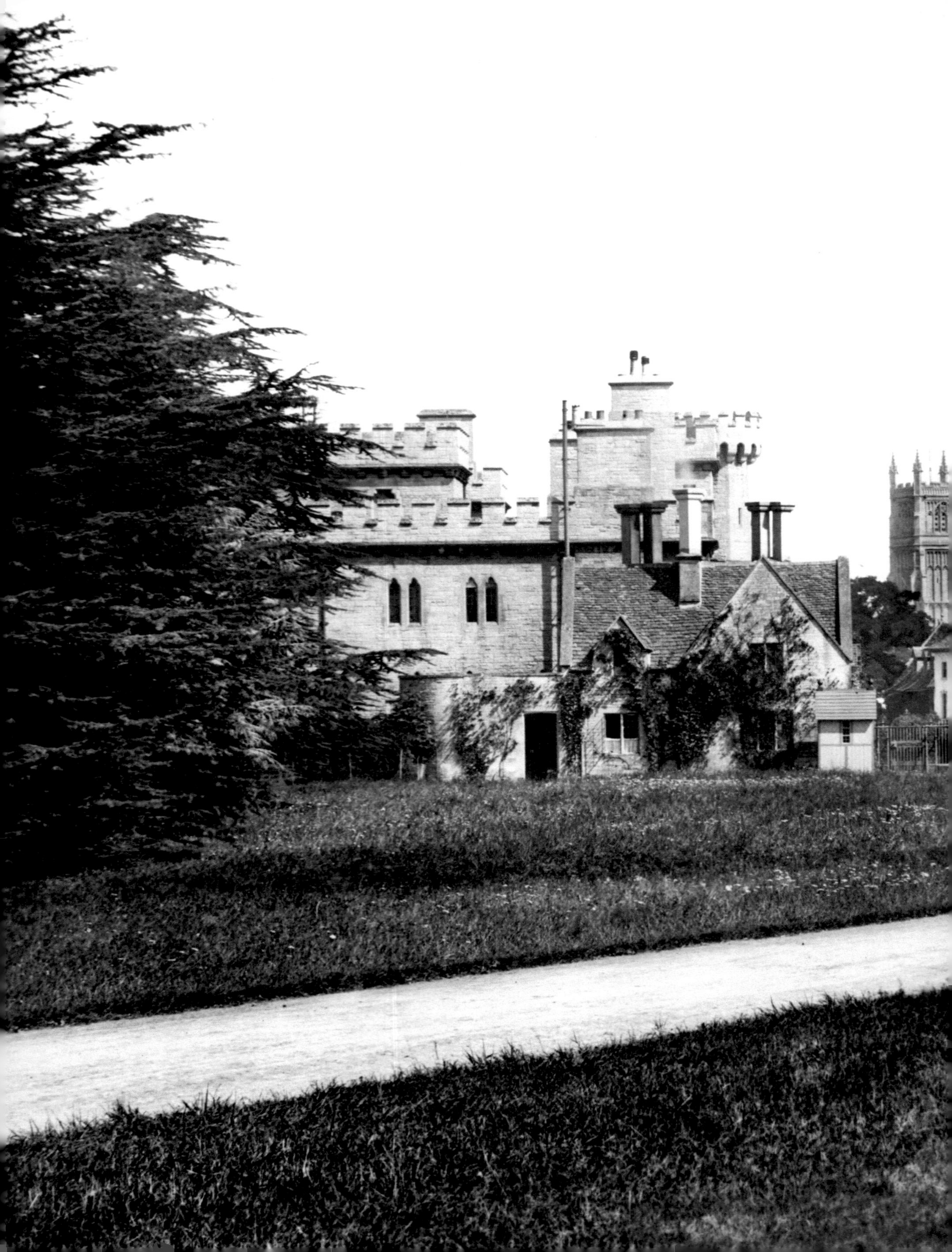

CHAPTER FIVE

*The Town Today:
Modern Life Built on
Ancient Foundations*

# CIRENCESTER – *a history and celebration of the town*

CIRENCESTER IS one of the top 20 market towns in the country - and that's official, because the 'Wilts and Gloucestershire Standard' says so! The town has a diversity of facilities to meet the needs of a new generation with a vastly different life-style, without ever losing the special something that gives a sense of belonging, unity and continuity - the ancient thread that weaves the ages together to strengthen the fabric of society. The paper published a summary of the survey by the Campaign to Protect Rural England in April 2004, in which it stated: 'Cirencester has been flagged up as an example of good practice and other towns [are] urged to follow suit.' Tribute was paid to Cirencester Park in particular, and the CPRE inspectors were impressed with the amount of green space in the town, together with the range of markets that are held on a regular basis, especially those which deal with local produce and craftwork.

## Wilts and Gloucestershire Standard

The first edition of the 'Wilts and Gloucestershire Standard' was published on 28 January 1837, as a four-page paper. Its opening column gave a dignified announcement to 'the Nobility, Gentry and Clergy and inhabitants, generally of the Counties of Wilts and Gloucester, that it would adhere to the Conservative cause'. The local effects of national change wrought through two world wars and the breaking down of the old social order are comprehensively illustrated in the paper's back issues. Today, the 'Standard' has no political bias; it is, as the editor says, a voice for the town, both as a forum for debate and as a champion of the community, fighting Cirencester's corner at regional and national level and spearheading campaigns on behalf of its readers.

**TOWN IN UK TOP 20 2004**
ZZZ00348 ('Wilts and Gloucestershire Standard')

The report was accompanied by a photograph of the Market Place, as viewed from the church tower.

**PETER DAVISON, EDITOR 2004**  ZZZ00349
(Wilts and Gloucestershire Standard)

The editor's commitment to support local causes often takes him from his desk into the community the paper serves.

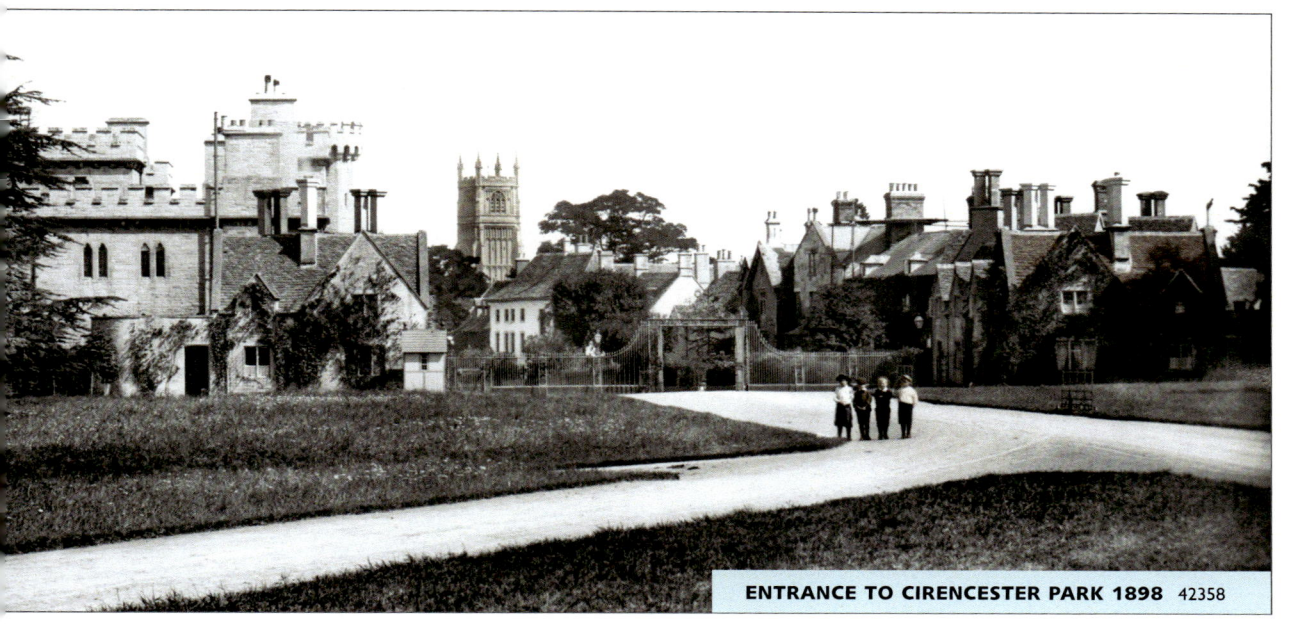

# The Town Today: Modern Life Built on Ancient Foundations

**ENTRANCE TO CIRENCESTER PARK 1898** 42358

The scene remains unchanged over a century later.

**GEORGE COLLICUT** ZZZ00343

(June Lewis-Jones)

A former editor, George Collicutt was awarded the MBE in the 1980s in recognition of his progressive leadership.

**RICHARD JEFFERIES** ZZZ00347

(Wilts and Gloucestershire Standard

Richard Jefferies, one-time reporter on the 'Standard, became a renowned writer on Victorian rural life.

**THE 'STANDARD' OFFICES 2004** C106713k (June Lewis-Jones)

The distinctive gabled front of the building still bears the word 'Printers' over the door - a reminder of the time when the paper was printed on site. The building on the left was the 'Bull Inn'.

# CIRENCESTER – *a history and celebration of the town*

**THE 'WILTS AND GLOUCESTERSHIRE' LOGO**
ZZZ00346

So, a millennium on from Domesday, the historic benchmark from which comparisons are often made, Cirencester is still true to its roots as a market town. Set in the shallows of the meandering Churn Valley within the Cotswolds, an area of outstanding natural beauty, it remains a forum for trading and commerce in diverse forms.

Market stalls still mushroom in the ancient Market Place. The Charter Market, which dates back a thousand years, is held on Monday and Friday of each week; the Farmers' Market, held on the second and fourth Saturday each month, brings local growers and producers together, giving shoppers the opportunity to discuss the source and production methods of their fare.

**CRICKLADE STREET c1960** C106103

The Midland Bank on the left replaced Bishop Brothers Family Grocers store about the time of the First World War.

## The Town Today: Modern Life Built on Ancient Foundations

**CRICKLADE STREET c1955** C106052

View towards the Market Place - a scene little changed in over 50 years.

**FARMERS' MARKET 2004** C106714k (June Lewis-Jones)

Stalls with home-made and local-grown food attract customers to the fortnightly market.

### Did you know?

Cirencester has one of the oldest charter markets in the country.

# CIRENCESTER – *a history and celebration of the town*

**THE MARKET PLACE c1960**  C106061

Stradlings clock, shown above the shuttered shop, was always known as 'the town clock'. Keen 'clock watchers' would compare its time with that shown on the nearby church clock.

Craft markets and antiques markets are held regularly in the Corn Hall, as well as a variety of specialist sales, ranging from rugs to books. And the ladies of the Women's Institute still tempt those who appreciate home-made cakes and bakes into the Ashcroft Centre every Friday morning. However, a future home for the long-established Cattle Market is still being considered in view of the present site being an option for the development of a new leisure centre. A more recent event is the annual Advent Market, when the town is literally lit up, with a celebrity of the day turning on the Christmas lights and everyone from the immediate area beating a path to Cirencester, the uncrowned Queen of the Cotswolds.

## Did you know?

*Cirencester can lay claim to one of, if not the, oldest open-air swimming pools in Britain.*

*The Town Today: Modern Life Built on Ancient Foundations* 109

**THE MARKET PLACE c1960** C106062

St John the Baptist is one of the largest parish churches in the country. Its tower, soaring some 40 metres (130 feet), is a distinctive landmark from all corners of the town.

**THE OPEN-AIR SWIMMING POOL 2004** C106715k

(June Lewis-Jones)

The open-air swimming pool was built in 1870 by the Bathurst family, and presented to the people of the town. With the battlemented bulk of the Old Barracks as a backdrop, it must rank as one of the most beautiful sites in the country. Over the last two decades the pool has been managed by a stalwart band of volunteers. Heated water, lifeguard training, swimming lessons and a whole range of improved facilities make this a popular place for all ages from May to September.

Indoor swimming is just one of the many activities on offer at the Cotswold Leisure Centre, and there is a wide range of facilities in the town for outdoor sports, from football, tennis and croquet to golf and bowls.

Cirencester Cricket Club has an idyllic, traditional English pitch at Cirencester Park, and just a little further afield is the world-famous polo ground where the cream of the polo teams can be seen at play throughout the summer months. The Park is a much-cherished asset to the town, a place where local people can walk or ride on horseback for miles in natural wooded parkland. This is where the crowds in their thousands flock to the internationally famous Cotswold Show and Country Fair each July, to enjoy, with more than a little patriotic and parochial pride, the best of local rural skills, crafts, produce and culture.

## Did you know?

*Cirencester Park is one of the largest in England in private ownership.*

The abbey grounds settle close to the town centre, spreading their open green spaces over the foundations of the once-so-powerful abbey. They are a tranquil haven for walkers and wildfowl, enlivened by the cheery chatter of children at play in the recreation area or music from the bandstand on a Sunday afternoon. St Michael's Park, adjoining Watermoor House, is the most recent of the three parks in Cirencester, and was redeveloped in 1984 to provide extra outdoor sporting and recreational facilities.

The annual Mop Fair bears little resemblance to its origins as a Hiring Fair, but carries on the tradition of what has always constituted 'all the fun of the fair' for changing generations. It is still held in the town centre.

**PRINCE CHARLES AND PRINCE WILLIAM AT POLO 2002**
ZZZ00342 (Michael Charity)

## The Town Today: Modern Life Built on Ancient Foundations

**BISHOPS WALK 2004** C106716k (June Lewis-Jones)

The colonnaded shopping arcade in Bishops Walk has a galleried café and bar above.

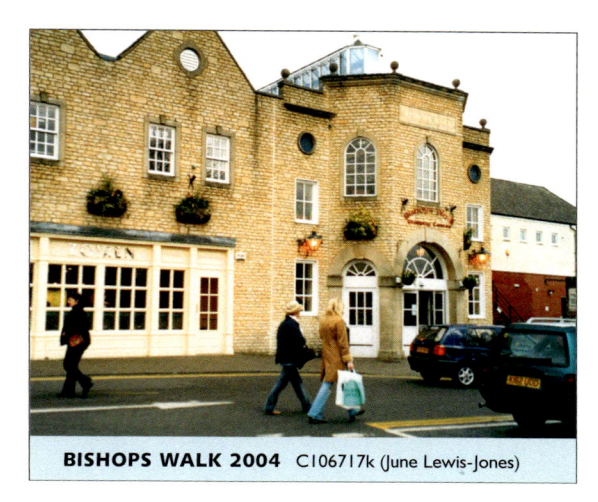

**BISHOPS WALK 2004** C106717k (June Lewis-Jones)

Bishops Walk links the Brewery car park with Cricklade Street. Note the name Zoiren (an old pronunciation of the abbreviation Ciren) on the shop.

Housing developments have sent out arterial branches into the once-fertile fields of farmland, with Victorian and Edwardian villas linking old thoroughfares. Modern flats have sprung up in the spaces in between, to accommodate the town's rapidly increased population. At close to 19,500 (according to the 2001 Census), the town has quadrupled in size since 1794, when it was estimated the figure stood at 4,000. The coming of the railway and improved travel and transport facilities increased that number to 5,500 in 1830. New schools and hospital and medical services have grown accordingly; and light industry and commercial and professional businesses employ many people from neighbouring villages as well as local people.

Although modern supermarkets now edge the town, the centre has grown organically within the ancient structure. A handful of long-established family businesses hold on to their proud tradition and are valued for their individuality and personal service. Visitors are always delighted to find attractive specialist shops and restaurants tucked away in intimate courtyards off the main streets.

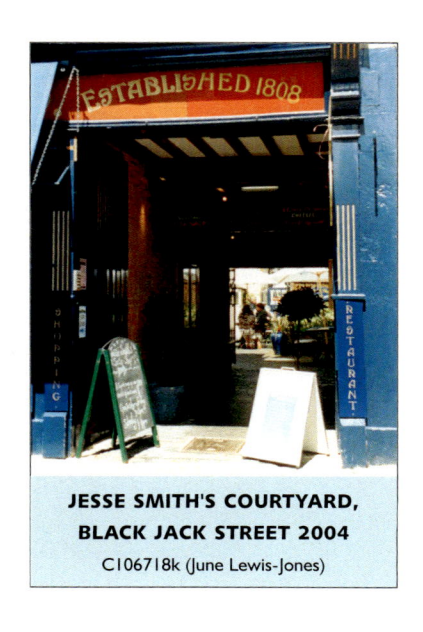

**JESSE SMITH'S COURTYARD, BLACK JACK STREET 2004**
C106718k (June Lewis-Jones)

Cosy al fresco eating in Jesse Smith's courtyard in Black Jack Street, with a splendid bistro in the former stables and a specialist cheese shop as close neighbour.

# CIRENCESTER – *a history and celebration of the town*

**BLACK JACK STREET c1955** C106009

A delightful enclave of small specialist shops and eating places just west of the church.

**BUTCHER'S BAGS**
ZZZ00340 & ZZZ00341

Jesse Smith established his business in 1808; its art nouveau front is a much-photographed feature of the town. The shop's bags proclaim that it was 'Voted Top Butcher's Shop of South West England'.

**SILVER STREET c1965** C106131

Links Castle Street to Park Street.

Cultural and social events punctuate Cirencester's calendar and offer a diversity of attractions, activities and entertainments in different venues - Bingham Hall and Library, the Phoenix Centre, the Parish Church, local schools, and the Sundial Theatre at Cirencester College (whose patron is Dame Judi Dench). These were joined in 1979 by the Brewery Arts Centre, which accommodates resident craftworkers, a coffee shop, an exhibition and activities centre, and a small theatre - in what had served the town for generations as a major brewery.

As well as all this, nowhere better exemplifies how the past influences the present and strengthens the ties of continuity than the Corinium Museum.

**BREWERY ARTS CENTRE 2004** C106719k (June Lewis-Jones)

The Brewery Arts Centre is a fine example of new life generated in an old building.

**OTTAKAR'S BOOKSHOP 2004**
C106720k (June Lewis-Jones)

Well-known figures in the literary field are often to be found at Ottakar's, giving a talk or signing their latest book. This row of shops is part of the rebuilding of the old Brewery Yard. The open space in front is an ideal display area for modern sculpture.

## The Corinium Museum

The Corinium Museum reopened in September 2004 after a major rebuilding project, with substantial financial backing from the Heritage Lottery Fund. It incorporates the original premises (in which the museum has been housed since 1938) within an expansive new building, laid out so as to give a walk through history from Palaeolithic times to the Lifelong Learning Centre of today. Electronically controlled seating allows for speedy conversion from lecture theatre to schoolroom to community room. Physical and intellectual access is at the heart of the new design. Visitors can experience and feel the grandeur that once was Roman Corinium, in a reconstruction of its complex cultural community. A wealthy town house complete with magnificent mosaic pavement contrasts with a lower-status strip house, floored with the cheaper opus signinum, a mixture of hydrated lime and crushed tile. It is revealing to find the Romans had a lot of the types of shops that we still have today - including take-aways! And 21st-century technology brings us a reconstructed likeness of a Saxon lady, possibly a princess - nicknamed Mrs Getty by the staff, because she was buried with more riches than any other female in the excavated Anglo-Saxon cemetery.

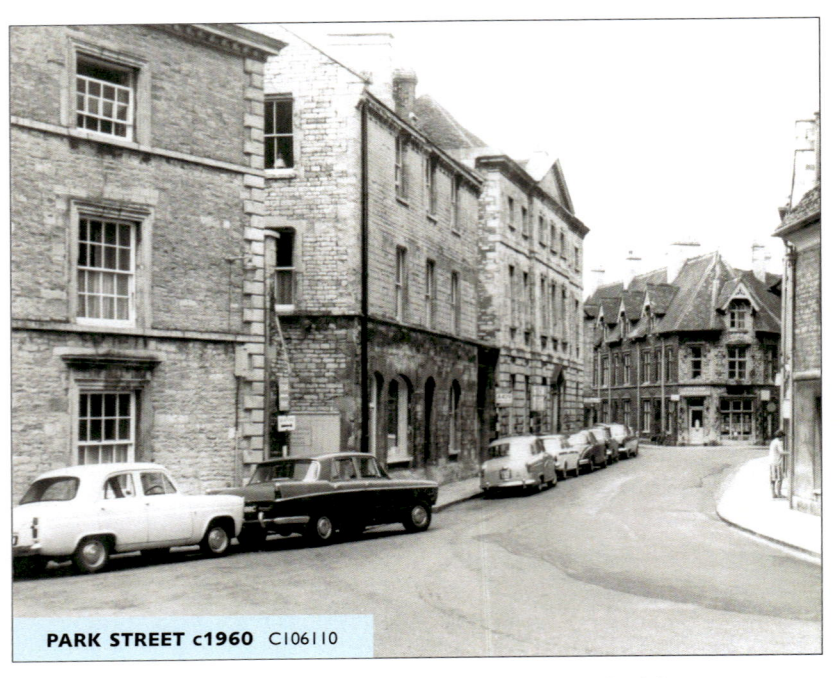

# CIRENCESTER – *a history and celebration of the town*

**PARK STREET c1960** C106110

The entrance to the Corinium Museum is just to the left of this view.

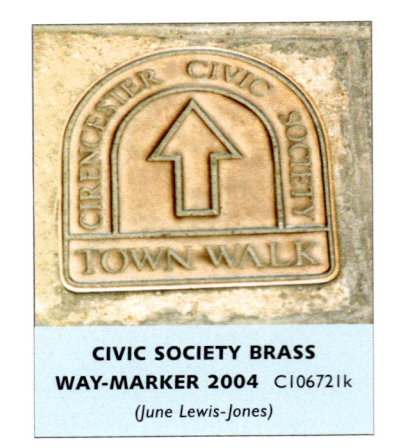

**CIVIC SOCIETY BRASS WAY-MARKER 2004** C106721k
*(June Lewis-Jones)*

A series of these markers is set into the pavement at various points, directing visitors on an exploratory town walk. Buildings of interest along the way can be identified by their distinctive blue plaque.

**ADVENT MARKET** ZZZ00345 ('Wilts and Gloucestershire Standard')

# The Jupiter Column

**RIGHT:** Judy Mills, Collections Management Officer, and Dr John Paddock, Museums Services Manager, overseeing the positioning of the famous Jupiter column - the first artefact to be installed during the Corinium rebuilding project. The exquisitely carved Bacchic capital was found in the abbey grounds in 1808. Dr Paddock says it would have been carved in the town, because Corinium had the finest school of sculptors in Roman Britain. It is now mounted on a stone column, as it would have been originally, for it was meant to be viewed from below.

**BELOW:** Detail from the design brief for the project, with the Jupiter capital on the Septimus Stone column as the focal point. It bears a unique inscription, providing evidence for the political division of fourth-century Roman Britain.

**ARTIST'S IMPRESSION OF THE ROMAN GALLERY** ZZZ00338
(courtesy of Corinium Museum)

**JUPITER COLUMN 2004** ZZZ00339
(June Lewis-Jones)

So today's scientific and artistic techniques weave together the threads of history to create a rich tapestry of Cirencester's life throughout the centuries, inspiring visitor and local alike to look anew at the town's built heritage and at the same time gain a palpable sense of progress into the new millennium.

## ACKNOWLEDGEMENTS

I wish to express my gratitude to all those who have been so helpful in providing information and material for this book, with particular thanks to:

Lord Apsley, for his interest and good wishes and the information on the Bathurst family and Cirencester Park Estate;

Bingham Library Staff;

Michael Charity, whose professional talent and status commended him as official photojournalist for royal visits to the region, for allowing me to use his photographs of their Royal Highnesses Prince Charles and Prince William, Diana the late Princess of Wales, and the Hon Bathurst family;

Mollie Coton, for the use of her personal collection on the work of her father, the late Lt Col Eric Cole, Architect;

Peter Davison, Editor of the 'Wilts and Gloucestershire Standard', for his good wishes, interest, and permission to reproduce copyright material;

Gloucestershire Record Office Staff;

Peter Grace, founder member of the Living Memory Historical Association;

Peter Holden, Tower Captain of Cirencester Bellringers;

Judy Mills, Collections Management Officer, for so generously giving me her time, sharing her expertise, and her enthusiastic preview of the major rebuilding and refurbishment of the Corinium Museum;

Lorna Parker, Archivist of the Royal Agricultural College, for historical background of the College and her time and interest in researching into the admission of George Harold Gibbs;

Ralph Smith, for his memories and photos and the use of the personal writings of his father, the late Edward Smith;

David Viner, whose historical knowledge of and interest in the heritage of his home town are without parallel, making his contribution and good wishes even the more valuable.

I also wish to acknowledge the assistance I have derived from the studies made on Cirencester by the late historian, Jean Welsford, and my use of the photos and old prints given to me many years ago by the late Phil Morse. Thanks also to Hilary Hainsworth for obtaining the Grammar School photo of 1935.

Other photographs were taken by me or are from my collection. If I have inadvertently infringed any copyright for images whose origins I cannot now trace or seek written permission for, I trust my apologies will be accepted. Thank you.

## BIBLIOGRAPHY

Alan McWhirr: Houses in Roman Cirencester, Alan Sutton 1986
Jean Welsford: Cirencester - A History and Guide, Alan Sutton 1991
Samuel Rudder: History of Cirencester 1780
Anthony Denning: Theatre in the Cotswolds, The Society for Theatre Research 1993
J Arthur Gibbs: A Cotswold Village, John Murray 1908
Mary Bliss and Mary Day: Cirencester Benefit Society 1890-1990, Alan Sutton 1990
Andrew Hignell and Adrian Thomas: 100 Great - Gloucestershire Cricket Club, TempusPublishing 2002
David J Viner: Cirencester As It Was, Hendon Publishing 1976
Jean Welsford and Peter Grace: Cirencester in the 1930s and 40s, Hendon Publishing 1990
Mike Oakley: Gloucestershire Railway Stations, The Dovecot Press 2003
June R Lewis: The Cotswolds At War, Alan Sutton 1992
June R Lewis: The Village School, Robert Hale 1989
Wilts and Gloucestershire Standard, passim

## FURTHER READING

David Verey: Cotswolds Churches, Batsford 1976
Alec Clifton-Taylor: Another Six English Towns, BBC Productions, London 1980
Jean Welsford: Cirencester in Old Photographs, Alan Sutton 1991
Keith Turner and Bryan Berkeley: A Narrow Cotswold Street, Coxwell Street Residents Association, Cirencester 2000
Kenneth J Beecham: History of Cirencester and the Roman City of Corinium 1887; Facsimile Reprint (with introduction by David Verey), Alan Sutton 1978
Alan McWhirr: Cirencester Excavations III, Alan Sutton 1986 (Corinium Museum)
David J Viner: The Thames and Severn Canal, Hendon Publishing 1977

## DEDICATION

To my husband, Ralph
For all the right reasons

# FRITH PRODUCTS & SERVICES

Francis Frith would doubtless be pleased to know that the pioneering publishing venture he started in 1860 still continues today. Over a hundred and forty years later, The Francis Frith Collection continues in the same innovative tradition and is now one of the foremost publishers of vintage photographs in the world. Some of the current activities include:

## INTERIOR DECORATION

Today Frith's photographs can be seen framed and as giant wall murals in thousands of pubs, restaurants, hotels, banks, retail stores and other public buildings throughout the country. In every case they enhance the unique local atmosphere of the places they depict and provide reminders of gentler days in an increasingly busy and frenetic world.

## PRODUCT PROMOTIONS

Frith products are used by many major companies to promote the sales of their own products or to reinforce their own history and heritage. Frith promotions have been used by Hovis bread, Courage beers, Scots Porage Oats, Colman's mustard, Cadbury's foods, Mellow Birds coffee, Dunhill pipe tobacco, Guinness, and Bulmer's Cider.

## GENEALOGY AND FAMILY HISTORY

As the interest in family history and roots grows world-wide, more and more people are turning to Frith's photographs of Great Britain for images of the towns, villages and streets where their ancestors lived; and, of course, photographs of the churches and chapels where their ancestors were christened, married and buried are an essential part of every genealogy tree and family album.

## FRITH PRODUCTS

All Frith photographs are available Framed or just as Mounted Prints and unmounted versions. These may be ordered from the address below. Other products available are - Calendars, Jigsaws, Canvas Prints, Mugs, Tea Towels, Tableware and local and prestige books.

## THE INTERNET

Over several hundred thousand Frith photographs can be viewed and purchased on the internet through the Frith websites!

For more detailed information on Frith products, look at
www.francisfrith.com

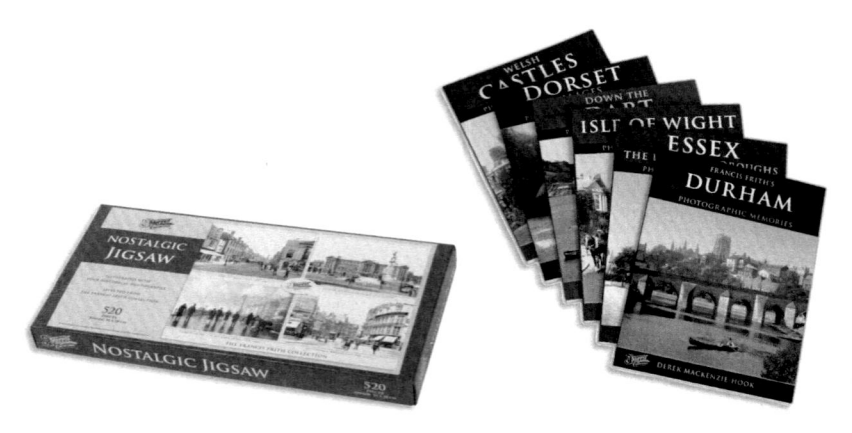

---

See the complete list of Frith Books at: www.francisfrith.com
This web site is regularly updated with the latest list of publications from The Francis Frith Collection. If you wish to buy books relating to another part of the country that your local bookshop does not stock, you may purchase on-line.

---

*For further information, trade, or author enquiries please contact us at the address below:*
The Francis Frith Collection, Unit 19 Kingsmead Business Park, Gillingham, Dorset SP8 5FB.
Tel: +44 (0)1722 716 376    Email: sales@francisfrith.co.uk

See Frith products on the internet at www.francisfrith.com

# FREE PRINT OF YOUR CHOICE
## CHOOSE A PHOTOGRAPH FROM THIS BOOK
+ POSTAGE

**Mounted Print**
*Overall size 14 x 11 inches (355 x 280mm)*

### TO RECEIVE YOUR FREE PRINT

**Choose any Frith photograph in this book**

Simply complete the Voucher opposite and return it with your payment (to cover postage and handling) and we will print the photograph of your choice in SEPIA (size 11 x 8 inches) and supply it in a cream mount ready to frame (overall size 14 x 11 inches).

**Order additional Mounted Prints at HALF PRICE - £19.00 each** (normally £38.00)

If you would like to order more Frith prints from this book, possibly as gifts for friends and family, you can buy them at half price (with no additional postage costs).

**Have your Mounted Prints framed**

For an extra £20.00 per print you can have your mounted print(s) framed in an elegant polished wood and gilt moulding, overall size 16 x 13 inches (no additional postage required).

---

**IMPORTANT!**

❶ Please note: aerial photographs and photographs with a reference number starting with a "Z" are not Frith photographs and cannot be supplied under this offer.

❷ Offer valid for delivery to one UK address only.

❸ These special prices are only available if you use this form to order. You must use the ORIGINAL VOUCHER on this page (no copies permitted). We can only despatch to one UK address.

❹ This offer cannot be combined with any other offer.

---

As a customer your name & address will be stored by Frith but not sold or rented to third parties. Your data will be used for the purpose of this promotion only.

*Send completed Voucher form to:*
**The Francis Frith Collection,
1 Chilmark Estate House, Chilmark,
Salisbury, Wiltshire SP3 5DU**

---

# *Voucher* for FREE and Reduced Price Frith Prints

*Please do not photocopy this voucher. Only the original is valid, so please fill it in, cut it out and return it to us with your order.*

| Picture ref no | Page no | Qty | Mounted @ £19.00 | Framed + £20.00 | Total Cost £ |
|---|---|---|---|---|---|
|  |  | 1 | Free of charge* | £ | £ |
|  |  |  | £19.00 | £ | £ |
|  |  |  | £19.00 | £ | £ |
|  |  |  | £19.00 | £ | £ |
|  |  |  | £19.00 | £ | £ |

*Please allow 28 days for delivery. Offer available to one UK address only*

* Post & handling £3.80

**Total Order Cost** £

Title of this book .................................

I enclose a cheque/postal order for £ ..........

made payable to 'The Francis Frith Collection'

OR please debit my Mastercard / Visa / Maestro card, details below

Card Number:

Issue No (Maestro only):     Valid from (Maestro):

Card Security Number:        Expires:

Signature:

Name Mr/Mrs/Ms .................................

Address .................................

.................................

.................................

......................... Postcode .................

Daytime Tel No .................................

Email .................................

Valid to 31/12/24

Free Print – see overleaf

### Can you help us with information about any of the Frith photographs in this book?

We are gradually compiling an historical record for each of the photographs in the Frith archive. It is always fascinating to find out the names of the people shown in the pictures, as well as insights into the shops, buildings and other features depicted.

If you recognize anyone in the photographs in this book, or if you have information not already included in the author's caption, do let us know. We would love to hear from you, and will try to publish it in future books or articles.

### An Invitation from The Francis Frith Collection to Share Your Memories

The 'Share Your Memories' feature of our website allows members of the public to add personal memories relating to the places featured in our photographs, or comment on others already added. Seeing a place from your past can rekindle forgotten or long held memories. Why not visit the website, find photographs of places you know well and add YOUR story for others to read and enjoy? We would love to hear from you!

**www.francisfrith.com/memories**

### Our production team

Frith books are produced by a small dedicated team at offices near Salisbury. Most have worked with the Frith Collection for many years. All have in common one quality: they have a passion for the Frith Collection.

### Frith Books and Gifts

We have a wide range of books and gifts available on our website utilising our photographic archive, many of which can be individually personalised.

**www.francisfrith.com**